Bootstrap Site Blueprints

Design mobile-first responsive websites with
Bootstrap 3

David Cochran

Ian Whitley

BIRMINGHAM - MUMBAI

Bootstrap Site Blueprints

Copyright © 2014 Packt Publishing

All rights reserved. No part of this book may be reproduced, stored in a retrieval system, or transmitted in any form or by any means, without the prior written permission of the publisher, except in the case of brief quotations embedded in critical articles or reviews.

Every effort has been made in the preparation of this book to ensure the accuracy of the information presented. However, the information contained in this book is sold without warranty, either express or implied. Neither the authors, nor Packt Publishing, and its dealers and distributors will be held liable for any damages caused or alleged to be caused directly or indirectly by this book.

Packt Publishing has endeavored to provide trademark information about all of the companies and products mentioned in this book by the appropriate use of capitals. However, Packt Publishing cannot guarantee the accuracy of this information.

First published: February 2014

Production Reference: 1140214

Published by Packt Publishing Ltd.
Livery Place
35 Livery Street
Birmingham B3 2PB, UK.

ISBN 978-1-78216-452-4

www.packtpub.com

Cover Image by Javier Rincon Borobia (javirbh@gmail.com)

Credits

Authors
David Cochran

Ian Whitley

Reviewers
Sampath Lokuge

Sohel Rana

Acquisition Editor
Sam Wood

Content Development Editor
Sweny M. Sukumaran

Technical Editors
Shweta S. Pant

Humera Shaikh

Nachiket Vartak

Copy Editors
Roshni Banerjee

Sarang Chari

Brandt D'Mello

Mradula Hegde

Project Coordinator
Amey Sawant

Proofreaders
Maria Gould

Paul Hindle

Indexer
Hemangini Bari

Production Coordinator
Aparna Bhagat

Cover Work
Aparna Bhagat

About the Authors

David Cochran serves as an Associate Professor of Communication at Oklahoma Wesleyan University. He has been teaching Interactive Design since 2005. A passion for best practices induced him to avoid shortcuts and hew towards web standards. When Twitter Bootstrap was first released in August 2011, he recognized it as a tool that would speed up development while supporting best practices. Thus, he began folding Bootstrap into his university courses, much to the benefit of his students.

In 2012, David produced a Bootstrap 2.0 tutorial series for webdesign.tutsplus.com. He also published a first short book about Bootstrap, *Twitter Bootstrap Web Development How-To*, *Packt Publishing*.

In his spare time, David blogs about web design at alittlecode.com. He also leads a media, design, and strategy company named BitBrilliant.

I would like to thank Oklahoma Wesleyan University for supporting this project and for providing a context for teaching and learning steeped in the Spirit of Christ. To my students, thank you for your excitement as we've learned new skills together. To Ian and my colleagues at BitBrilliant, thank you for joining me in the good work of building better web interfaces for great clients and good causes. To my wife, Julie, and our children, thank you for your patience through this process—and for your good humor, encouragement, and fun. I'm grateful.

Ian Whitley developed a passion for writing and literature at a young age. In 2010, he developed a deep interest in web development and decided to get involved in it. When the opportunity to help write a book on web development came up, it seemed like too good of an offer to pass up. He was one of the early adopters of Twitter Bootstrap when it was first released in 2011. With the help of David Cochran, he quickly conquered the system and has used it for many different web projects. Currently, he uses Bootstrap in relation to WordPress, using both in conjunction to create custom and creative solutions for his client.

Living in the Bartlesville, OK, Ian is the lead developer for BitBrilliant, the company that David Cochran founded. He is always looking to further his skills—both for the web and in the many hobbies he pursues, which include leather working and writing.

I would like to thank everyone I work with at BitBrilliant for being so helpful during this entire writing process and for being such great co-workers and friends. I would also like to thank my parents, Colin and Jackie Whitley, for providing me with a wonderful education, guiding me in my faith in Jesus Christ, and teaching me the skills I needed to make it in this life. I would not be who I am without your guidance.

About the Reviewers

Sampath Lokuge is currently working as a Technical Lead at a well known software consulting company in Sri Lanka. He holds a Bachelor of Science degree in Mathematics and Computer Science from the University of Colombo, Sri Lanka.

Sampath possesses over six years of experience in constructing web applications using Microsoft technologies such as ASP.net MVC, C#, SQL Server, Web API, Entity Framework, and also other web technologies such as HTML5, CSS3, and jQuery. He has earned Microsoft certifications such as MCP, MCAD, MCSD, and MCTS. Very recently, he has completed an MS (Microsoft Specialist) in MVC 4, HTML5, and CSS3 with JavaScript.

Besides that, he is an active blogger and he writes about web and mobile development issues and promoting best practices. You can visit his technical blog at `http://sampathloku.blogspot.com/`.

He also actively participates in online communities such as Code Project and StackOverflow. He handles two communities, which are ASP.net MVC 5 With C# on Linkedin and EntityFramework 6 on G+. He is a Buddhist and a vegetarian.

I would like to thank my mother who supported me in completing my reviews on time and with good quality.

Sohel Rana has been working in the IT industry for almost eight years, with working experience in Asia, Europe, and Australia. He's involved in architecting, designing, and developing large Enterprise Solutions using different types of Microsoft-based technologies such as ASP.net, Dot Net Nuke, Ektrone, and SharePoint.

Currently, Sohel is working as a Senior SharePoint Consultant at NEC IT in Perth, Australia. He has achieved Microsoft Most Valuable Professional (MVP) twice for his contribution to the SharePoint community. He's a regular blogger on SharePoint, and you can find his blog just by googling Sohel SharePoint. He loves to explore new technologies.

www.PacktPub.com

Support files, eBooks, discount offers, and more

You might want to visit www.PacktPub.com for support files and downloads related to your book.

Did you know that Packt offers eBook versions of every book published, with PDF and ePub files available? You can upgrade to the eBook version at www.PacktPub.com and as a print book customer, you are entitled to a discount on the eBook copy. Get in touch with us at service@packtpub.com for more details.

At www.PacktPub.com, you can also read a collection of free technical articles, sign up for a range of free newsletters and receive exclusive discounts and offers on Packt books and eBooks.

http://PacktLib.PacktPub.com

Do you need instant solutions to your IT questions? PacktLib is Packt's online digital book library. Here, you can access, read and search across Packt's entire library of books.

Why subscribe?

- Fully searchable across every book published by Packt
- Copy and paste, print and bookmark content
- On demand and accessible via web browser

Free access for Packt account holders

If you have an account with Packt at www.PacktPub.com, you can use this to access PacktLib today and view nine entirely free books. Simply use your login credentials for immediate access.

Table of Contents

Preface

Since its debut in August 2011, Twitter Bootstrap, now simply Bootstrap, has become by far the most popular framework for empowering and enhancing frontend web design. With Version 3, Bootstrap reaches an exciting new milestone, introducing a mobile-first responsive grid, new and powerful LESS mixins, and a lean code base optimized for modern browsers.

This book is a hands-on guide to the inner workings of Bootstrap. In an easy-to-follow, step-by-step format, you'll experience the power of customizing and recompiling Bootstrap's LESS files and adapting Bootstrap's JavaScript plugins to design professional user interfaces.

At the end of the day, this book is about something bigger than Bootstrap. Bootstrap is but a tool—a means to an end. By the end of this book, you will become a more adept and efficient web designer.

What this book covers

Chapter 1, Getting Started with Bootstrap, teaches us how to download Bootstrap, set up a site template based on the HTML5 Boilerplate, and practice compiling Bootstrap's LESS files to CSS.

Chapter 2, Bootstrappin' Your Portfolio, helps us to build a basic portfolio site with a full-width carousel, three columns of text, and social icons provided by Font Awesome—customizing Bootstrap's LESS files and adding your own in the process.

Chapter 3, Bootstrappin' a WordPress Theme, enables us to take the portfolio design from *Chapter 2, Bootstrappin' Your Portfolio*, and turn it into a WordPress theme. We'll start with the excellent Roots Theme and customize template files, LESS, CSS, and JavaScript to suit our needs.

Chapter 4, Bootstrappin' Business, shows us how to create a complex banner area, add dropdown menus and utility navigation, build a complex three-column page layout, and add a four-column footer, and ensures that all these things remain fully responsive!

Chapter 5, Bootstrappin' E-commerce, guides us through the design of a products page capable of managing multiple rows of products in a complex responsive grid. While at it, we will provide a fully responsive design for options to filter products by category, brand, and so on.

Chapter 6, Bootstrappin' a One-page Marketing Website, gives a detailed outline of how to design a beautiful one-page scrolling website with a large welcome message, a grid of product features with large icons, customer testimony in a masonry layout, and a set of three thoughtfully designed pricing tables.

Appendix A, Optimizing Site Assets, walks us through the essential process for optimizing Bootstrap LESS/CSS and JavaScript for production, using the portfolio results from *Chapter 2, Bootstrappin' Your Portfolio* as an example. This will help you in all Bootstrap projects.

Appendix B, Implementing Responsive Images, includes the process of implementing the leading responsive images solution, Picturefill, in the home page carousel for the portfolio site in *Chapter 2, Bootstrappin' Your Portfolio*, which you can use in all your future projects.

Appendix C, Adding Swipe to the Carousel, describes the process of implementing a leading plugin for adding swipe functionality, `Hammer.js`, to the Bootstrap carousel.

What you need for this book

To complete the exercises in this book, you will need the following software:

- A modern web browser (Internet Explorer 8 or newer)
- A code editor
- A LESS compiler with `less.js` updated to at least Version 1.3.3

Who this book is for

This book is assumed to be good for readers who are comfortable with hand-coding HTML and CSS and are familiar with the fundamentals of valid HTML5 markup and well-structured stylesheets. Basic familiarity with JavaScript is a bonus, as we will be making use of Bootstrap's jQuery plugins. We will work a great deal with LESS to customize, compose, and compile stylesheets. Those who are familiar with LESS will gain significant experience working with the details of Bootstrap's LESS files. Those who are new to LESS will find this book a reasonably thorough primer.

Conventions

In this book, you will find a number of styles of text that distinguish between different kinds of information. Here are some examples of these styles, and an explanation of their meaning.

Code words in text, database table names, folder names, filenames, file extensions, pathnames, dummy URLs, user input, and Twitter handles are shown as follows: "less/bootstrap/navbar.less".

A block of code is set as follows:

```
<FilesMatch "\.(ttf|otf|eot|woff)$">
  <IfModule mod_headers.c>
    Header set Access-Control-Allow-Origin "*"
  </IfModule>
</FilesMatch>
```

New terms and **important words** are shown in bold. Words that you see on the screen, in menus or dialog boxes for example, appear in the text like this: "Once there, the large **Download source** button is your friend."

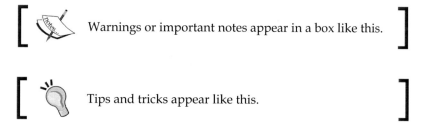

Warnings or important notes appear in a box like this.

Tips and tricks appear like this.

Reader feedback

Feedback from our readers is always welcome. Let us know what you think about this book—what you liked or may have disliked. Reader feedback is important for us to develop titles that you really get the most out of.

To send us general feedback, simply send an e-mail to feedback@packtpub.com, and mention the book title via the subject of your message.

If there is a topic that you have expertise in and you are interested in either writing or contributing to a book, see our author guide on www.packtpub.com/authors.

Customer support

Now that you are the proud owner of a Packt book, we have a number of things to help you to get the most from your purchase.

Downloading the example code

You can download the example code files for all Packt books you have purchased from your account at http://www.packtpub.com. If you purchased this book elsewhere, you can visit http://www.packtpub.com/support and register to have the files e-mailed directly to you.

Errata

Although we have taken every care to ensure the accuracy of our content, mistakes do happen. If you find a mistake in one of our books—maybe a mistake in the text or the code—we would be grateful if you would report this to us. By doing so, you can save other readers from frustration and help us improve subsequent versions of this book. If you find any errata, please report them by visiting http://www.packtpub.com/submit-errata, selecting your book, clicking on the **errata submission form** link, and entering the details of your errata. Once your errata are verified, your submission will be accepted and the errata will be uploaded on our website, or added to any list of existing errata, under the Errata section of that title. Any existing errata can be viewed by selecting your title from http://www.packtpub.com/support.

Piracy

Piracy of copyright material on the Internet is an ongoing problem across all media. At Packt, we take the protection of our copyright and licenses very seriously. If you come across any illegal copies of our works, in any form, on the Internet, please provide us with the location address or website name immediately so that we can pursue a remedy.

Please contact us at copyright@packtpub.com with a link to the suspected pirated material.

We appreciate your help in protecting our authors, and our ability to bring you valuable content.

Questions

You can contact us at questions@packtpub.com if you are having a problem with any aspect of the book, and we will do our best to address it.

1
Getting Started with Bootstrap

Bootstrap's popularity as a frontend web development framework is easy to understand. It provides a palette of user-friendly, cross-browser tested solutions for most standard UI conventions. Its ready-made, community-tested combination of HTML markup, CSS styles, and JavaScript behaviors greatly speeds up the task of developing a frontend web interface, and it yields a pleasing result out of the gate. With the fundamental elements quickly in place, we can customize the design on top of a solid foundation.

But not all that is popular, efficient, and effective is good. Too often, a handy tool can generate and reinforce bad habits; not so with Bootstrap, at least not necessarily so. Those who have watched it from the beginning know that its first release and early updates have occasionally favored pragmatic efficiency over best practices. The fact is that some best practices, right from semantic markup to mobile-first design to performance-optimized assets, require extra time and effort to implement.

Quantity and quality

If handled well, I will suggest that Bootstrap is a boon for the web development community in terms of quality as well as efficiency. Since developers are attracted to the web development framework, they become part of a coding community that draws them increasingly into current best practices. From the start, Bootstrap has encouraged implementation of tried, tested, and future-friendly CSS solutions, from Nicholas Galagher's CSS normalize to CSS3's displacement of image-heavy design elements. It has also supported (if not always modeled) HTML5 semantic markup.

Improving with age

With the release of v2.0, Bootstrap helped take responsive design into the mainstream, ensuring that its interface elements could travel well across devices, from desktops to tablets to handhelds.

Now, with its v3.0 release, Bootstrap has stepped up its game again by providing the following features:

- The responsive grid is now mobile-first friendly
- Icons now utilize web fonts and are thus mobile- and retina-friendly
- With the drop of support for IE7, markup and CSS conventions are now leaner and more efficient

The power of leaner CSS

In addition, there is the power of **Leaner CSS (LESS)** to consider. When we move beyond merely applying classes to markup and take the next step to dig in and customize Bootstrap's LESS files, we gain tremendous power and efficiency. Starting with a solid basis using Bootstrap's default styles, we can move on to innovate and customize to our heart's content.

In other words, Bootstrap is a powerful resource. I intend to help you leverage it in exciting and serious ways, working with efficiency, adhering to best practices, and producing beautiful, user-friendly interfaces.

Downloading Bootstrap

There are many ways to download Bootstrap, but not all ways of downloading Bootstrap are equal. For what follows, we must be sure to get the LESS files as these files give us the power to customize and innovate upon Bootstrap's underlying style rules. For this exercise, we'll go straight to the source, that is, GetBootstrap.com.

Once there, the large **Download source** button is your friend. At least as of Version 3.0.2, this is the second large button on the homepage of GetBootstrap.com.

In case something should change, you can always follow the **GitHub project** link, and once at the GitHub repository, click on the **Download ZIP** button.

The files you'll have

Once you've downloaded the Bootstrap source files, you should see a file structure that is similar to the following screenshot:

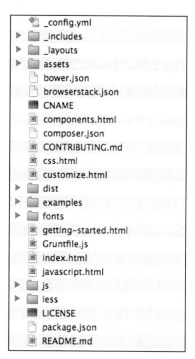

Admittedly, that's a lot of files, and we don't need them all. On the plus side, we have everything we want from Bootstrap.

While the exact contents of the repository will change over time, the main contents will remain relatively consistent. Most notably, in the **less** folder, you will find all the important LESS files, which are key to every project in this book. Another benefit is that the **js** folder contains Bootstrap's individual JavaScript plugins so that these may be selectively included as needed.

On the other hand, if you want Bootstrap's default precompiled CSS or JavaScript files (such as `bootstrap.css` or `bootstrap.min.js`), those are still available within the **dist** folder. As a bonus, you'll find the example HTML templates in the **examples** folder. In fact, we'll use one of these examples to set up our first project template folder.

Preparing a project template folder

Let's create a folder with the essential files we'll need to launch a project. We'll use the excellent **HTML5 Boilerplate** (**H5BP**) for our starting point, folding Bootstrap's files in their appropriate places.

Getting H5BP

Navigate to `h5bp.com` in your browser, a short link that will redirect you to H5BP's main documentation page. You may download the H5BP files directly from this page or from the linked GitHub project by clicking on the **SOURCE CODE** tab available at `h5bp.com`.

Extract the ZIP file and rename the folder to `Project Template 1`.

Inside this folder, you'll find the file and folder structure as shown in the following screenshot:

If your file system does not show hidden files, you will not see the .htaccess file. In my case, I have used my FTP browser to navigate to my local folder to make the .htaccess file visible.

Deleting unnecessary Boilerplate files

Delete the following folders and files, which are specific only to H5BP:

- The css folder because we'll soon create our own CSS files using LESS
- CHANGELOG.md
- CONTRIBUTING.md
- The doc folder and its contents

Evaluating the Boilerplate .htaccess file

If you have not read about the H5BP's .htaccess file before, you should take a look at the H5BP documentation, which is featured prominently at http://h5bp. com. In addition, the file itself is very well commented. Open it in your editor and read through it. Depending on your hosting setup and the needs of your site, you may or may not need all or a part of what this file does. Part of the purpose of what's in this file is to maximum site performance. Take it seriously, consult wise advice, and decide accordingly. In my case, my hosting provider handles these things, and so I don't need the .htaccess file.

Updating required Boilerplate files

The following files provide standard information about your project. They may be updated and used, if desired, or you may leave them out. It's up to you.

- humans.txt: This file assigns appropriate credits to you, H5BP, Bootstrap, and any other contributors.
- LICENSE.md: Prior to the H5BP license, add your own desired licensing information for the website you'll build with this license. After H5BP's license, add the licensing information for Bootstrap and other libraries that play a significant role in your end product.
- README.md: Update this file to provide a basic orientation to the entire project.

Updating the favicon and touch icons

Remember to replace the Boilerplate's default icon images with your desired images for your project. These include the following icon images:

- `apple-touch-icon-precomposed.png`
    - For best results across all mobile devices, including high-pixel-density screens, this should be 144px square (or 152px as in the Boilerplate version).

- `favicon.ico`
    - A 32px square icon image.

 Previous versions of the Boilerplate once included as many as six sizes of touch icons. Recently, this strategy was re-evaluated. Because the large icon will be used by all relevant devices, and the performance hit is very very small, it has been decided to reduce development overhead and have only one touch icon. For the discussion, see `https://github.com/h5bp/html5-boilerplate/issues/1367#ref-pullrequest-18787780`.

Pulling in the Bootstrap files

We are ready to pull Bootstrap's files into our `Project Template 1` folder and file structure. We'll move down through the big Bootstrap repository, selecting out only the parts we need. To speed up this process, I highly recommend having your Bootstrap 3 files open in one file browser window and your project template files open in another to facilitate comparing, dragging, and dropping.

Fonts

From the main `Bootstrap` folder, copy the `fonts` folder, and paste it into the main directory of your `Project Template 1` folder. This contains the important **Glyphicon** fonts that come with Bootstrap. (If you've not used font icons before, you're in for a treat.)

For good measures, I'm going to suggest that you add a cross-domain-friendly `.htaccess` file to this folder. Why? As more hosting services provide **Content Delivery Network** (**CDN**) for your site's static assets, you may discover, as I have, that some browsers refuse to recognize your web fonts without this access file. (Note that the H5BP `.htaccess` file contains lines to take care of this. The step we are taking now is aimed at ensuring that we do not run into problems even if the H5BP `.htaccess` file is not in the root directory of the site.)

Create a new file in your code editor, and add the following lines:

```
<FilesMatch "\.(ttf|otf|eot|woff)$">
  <IfModule mod_headers.c>
    Header set Access-Control-Allow-Origin "*"
  </IfModule>
</FilesMatch>
```

>
> **Downloading the example code**
>
> You can download the example code files for all Packt books you have purchased from your account at http://www.packtpub.com. If you purchased this book elsewhere, you can visit http://www.packtpub.com/support and register to have the files e-mailed directly to you.

Save the newly created file directly inside the `fonts` folder naming it `.htaccess`. (Note that if you're working locally, your OS may make the file invisible. If you have trouble getting your OS to make hidden files visible, you can often view it again by using your FTP client, setting its preferences to view hidden files, and using it to navigate to this folder.)

Once in place, the `.htaccess` file travels with your `fonts` folder, ensuring that your web fonts work in all browsers across whichever hosting and CDN services your websites may use.

JavaScript

Now let's try to bring in Bootstrap's JavaScript. Thanks to the HTML5 Boilerplate, we already have a JavaScript folder (named `js`) in place. Inside this, you'll find four files, two of them inside a subfolder named `vendor`, as shown in the following screenshot:

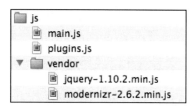

Bootstrap's plugins make use of jQuery, and the Boilerplate has it ready for us. Alongside jQuery, you'll see the Modernizr script. If you're unfamiliar with Modernizr, it includes an HTML5 shiv, which enables HTML5 sectioning elements in Internet Explorer 8. We're supporting IE8 in these projects, and so we need this here. In addition, Modernizr enables us to test for specific browser capabilities easily, such as CSS 3D transforms (to read more, see `http://modernizr.com/docs/`). We'll use Modernizr's feature-detection powers in the last chapter of the book.

Now, we need to add Bootstrap's plugins to the mix. First, let's bring them over as a group of individual plugins. Inside the main `js` folder of your `Project Template 1` folder, create a subfolder named `bootstrap`. Now copy into this the files you'll find in Bootstrap's `js` folder. The following are the Bootstrap's plugins, each as an individual file:

By copying and pasting these plugins into your new `js/bootstrap` folder, when you're ready to optimize your site for performance, you can select just the plugins you need, thereby eliminating the others and reducing file size.

Meanwhile, it may be helpful to have all of Bootstrap's plugins available during the development phase. That way, if you need to add an accordion, a tooltip, or a carousel, you can do it at your whim. Let's do this for ourselves now.

The H5BP method of doing this is to paste the code for all plugins into the provided `plugins.js` template file. This is a best practice when we're finished and ready to optimize the site because fewer HTTP requests means faster site loading times. (Loading one file of, say, 80 KB is more efficient than loading four files of 20 KB each.)

While developing, it's fairly convenient to use this same structure. It simply requires that we copy and paste the code for our required plugins into the `plugins.js` file. Let's find Bootstrap's big file of plugins and do this here.

You may prefer to work otherwise during the development stage, adding links to individual plugins to your markup during development, and then rolling the plugins into one minified file at the end. If you prefer that method, you can ignore this set of instructions and replace them with your own steps.

From Bootstrap's main folder, navigate to the `dist` folder to find the distribution files. Here, in the `js` folder, are `bootstrap.js` and `bootstrap.min.js`, containing all of Bootstrap's plugins rolled into one fat file. We will not be editing the plugins in these exercises, so let's use the minified version.

Once you've found it, perform the following steps:

1. Open `bootstrap.min.js` in your editor.
2. Copy the code, including the comment at the top. (Select all, then copy.)
3. Now, open `plugins.js` from your new project files.
4. Paste Bootstrap's plugin code inside the file, below the `// Place any jQuery/helper plugins in here.` comment. So, you'll now see something like the following:

```
// Place any jQuery/helper plugins in here.

/**
 * bootstrap.js v3.0.0 by @fat and @mdo
 * Copyright 2013 Twitter Inc.
 * http://www.apache.org/licenses/LICENSE-2.0
 */
if(!jQuery)throw new Error("Bootstrap requires
jQuery");+function(a){"use strict";
...
```

And of course the rest of the lengthy block of code will follow.

5. Save and exit.

You now have Bootstrap's plugins loaded and ready!

By keeping the comments from the top of Bootstrap's plugins, as well as from any other plugins we may include down the line, we are giving credit where credit is due and including essential licensing information. We're also making it easier for ourselves to search and sort through our plugins later. For instance, while optimizing the following projects for production, you'll want to substitute minified versions of only the specific Bootstrap plugins you'll be using in the project. Keeping these comments in place will help greatly at that point.

Holding off on the CSS

In the later projects, we are going to create a custom version of the Bootstrap CSS using LESS. We'll be doing this early in the next chapter, so hold on.

Bringing the LESS files over

Let's bring over all the important Bootstrap LESS files. Copy the `bootstrap/less` folder to the main directory of your `Project Template 1` folder.

Taking inventory

The main folder of your `Project Template 1` folder should now look like the following screenshot:

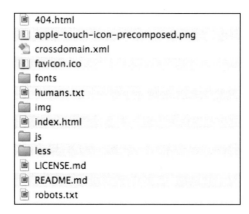

Your `fonts` folder, with the new `.htaccess` file within it, should contain the following files:

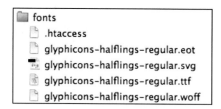

 I've used my FTP client to view these files, and set it to show hidden files. You may not be able to see your `.htaccess` file without taking similar steps.

The `img` folder should be empty, as was the H5BP folder from which it came.

The `js` folder should contain the following subfolders and files:

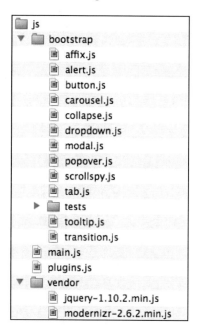

Because of its modular approach, Bootstrap's `less` folder contains a long list of files. We'll double-check these as we prepare to compile them in the forthcoming sections.

First, let's set up an HTML file.

Setting up the HTML template file

From your new project folder, open `index.html` in your editor. This sample markup file came with H5BP and contains several best practices and recommendations within it. We'll build on this basis and integrate it with our Bootstrap workflow. First, let's take a moment to note what's in it.

Scanning down through the file, you'll notice several interesting features. These are clearly explained in the H5BP documentation. You may easily get there from `http://h5bp.com`, but let me briefly run through a few of the features here. You'll see them in the following order:

- The HTML5 doctype:

  ```
  <!DOCTYPE html>
  ```

- Conditional comments for Internet Explorer, which enable developers to compose fixes for older IE browsers using appropriate nested selectors:

  ```
  <!--[if lt IE 7]><html class="no-js lt-ie9 lt-ie8 lt-ie7">
    <![endif]-->
  <!--[if IE 7]><html class="no-js lt-ie9 lt-ie8"><![endif]--
    >
  <!--[if IE 8]><html class="no-js lt-ie9"><![endif]-->
  <!--[if gt IE 8]><!--><html class="no-js"><!--<![endif]-->
  ```

- The `html` tag also has a class of `no-js`. If a browser's JavaScript is enabled, this class will be removed by the Modernizr script (referenced in the preceding part of this chapter) and replaced with the class `js`. If it is not removed, it signals that JavaScript is not enabled, and we may craft CSS rules for such cases using nested selectors.

- You'll see meta tags for the following things:
  - Specifying the character set as follows:

    ```
    <meta charset="utf-8">
    ```

  - Instructing an IE browser to use the most updated version of its rendering engine, or to use Google's Chrome Frame if it is installed as follows:

    ```
    <meta http-equiv="X-UA-Compatible"
      content="IE=edge,chrome=1">
    ```

  - The description tag for providing a description of the site is as follows:

    ```
    <meta name="description" content="">
    ```

- ○ A mobile-friendly viewport meta tag will be as follows:

```
<meta name="viewport" content="width=device-width">
```

- In place of links to a favicon or touch icon, you'll find a comment recommending that we simply place the icons in the site's root directory, where they will automatically be found by the users' browsers and devices.

- You'll see two stylesheet links — one to `normalize.css` and another to `main.css` — as follows:

```
<link rel="stylesheet" href="css/normalize.css">
<link rel="stylesheet" href="css/main.css">
```

- Then, you will see a script tag loading the Modernizr script. This needs to be loaded here in order for the HTML5 shiv it contains to equip IE8 so that it recognizes the HTML5 sectioning elements.

```
<script src="js/vendor/modernizr-2.6.2.min.js"></script>
```

- Then there is an IE conditional comment, with a message recommending the users of older IE browsers to upgrade to a more modern browser.

```
<!--[if lt IE 7]>
  <p class="chromeframe">You are using an
    <strong>outdated</strong> browser. ...
<![endif]-->
```

- A single paragraph of content text.

- A link to Google's hosted version of jQuery, followed by a link to a local fallback copy of jQuery:

```
<script src="//ajax.googleapis.com/ajax/libs/jquery/1.10.2/
  jquery.min.js"></script>
<script>window.jQuery || document.write('<script
  src="js/vendor/jquery-1.10.2.min.js">
  <\/script>')</script>
```

- Links to `plugins.js` and `main.js`, which are intended to hold the code for JavaScript plugins (in `plugins.js`) and your custom code (in `main.js`):

```
<script src="js/plugins.js"></script>
<script src="js/main.js"></script>
```

- The Google Analytics script:

```
<script>
  var _gaq=[['_setAccount','UA-XXXXX-
    X'],['_trackPageview']];
  (function(d,t){var g=d.createElement(t),
```

```
         s=d.getElementsByTagName(t)[0];
       g.src=('https:'==location.protocol?'//ssl':'//www')+'
         .google-analytics.com/ga.js';
       s.parentNode.insertBefore(g,s)}(document,'script'));
     </script>
```

If you wish to know more about the reason and purpose for any of these elements, I would encourage you to take some time to read through the H5BP HTML documentation (see `https://github.com/h5bp/html5-boilerplate/blob/v4.3.0/doc/html.md`), where these lines are clearly explained with references.

For our purposes, we will perform the following operations on the elements of this template:

1. We'll give our site a title. We'll update the legacy IE conditional comment for users of old browsers.
2. We'll compile Bootstrap's CSS from the LESS files. We'll add some basic page content.
3. We'll integrate Bootstrap's JavaScript plugins and ensure that the responsive navbar works as it should.

Once we've done the these things, we'll have everything in place to begin building our designs.

Giving your site a title

Take a moment to update `index.html` by giving it a title that fits this project. You can call your portfolio whatever you'd like to. I'll call mine as `Bootstrappin' Portfolio`. For the sake of precision, I'll use the HTML entity `&#39;` for the apostrophe, as shown in the following line of code:

```
<title>Bootstrappin&#39; Portfolio</title>
```

Adjusting the outdated browser message

The file carries a message for users of ancient browsers. You'll find this right around line 20. It reads as follows:

```
You are using an outdated browser. Please upgrade your browser
or activate Google Chrome Frame to improve your experience.
```

Note that it includes links to `http://browsehappy.com`, which features recommended browser upgrades, and to the Google Chrome Frame, a free plugin to retrofit Internet Explorer with modern browser capabilities. (Note that the Google Chrome Frame reference may go away after Google stops supporting it in January 2014.)

At the time of writing this book, this message came wrapped in a conditional comment that targets only Internet Explorer browsers older than IE7 (thus, IE6, IE5, and so on). No one else will see this message unless, of course, they view the source code.

Meanwhile, the world is pressing on. Many organizations are upgrading browsers, and many designers are dropping or reducing support for IE7. Typically, the goal is to ensure that IE7 users can navigate through the site and gain access to its information, though they will not have the full experience.

The reason for this is pretty pragmatic. Fully supporting IE7 requires writing a number of workarounds, both in CSS and in JavaScript, at the cost of more code, more bandwidth, more time, and more money.

Thus, Bootstrap 3 has dropped support for IE7. When we're done developing, we should test to ensure nothing restricts IE7 users from reading and navigating through our site. However, they won't see its full beauty.

So, let's update the message to include IE7 users. We need to change the opening tag of the conditional comment by adding an e for = , so that it reads the following:

```
<!--[if lte IE 7]>
```

Note that it now says `lte` where originally it was only `lt`.

A few notes seem in order.

> For IE7 and older browsers, you might consider providing basic styles in a legacy stylesheet to ensure these users can utilize your site.
>
> If you have a large base of users who rely on IE7 and who are unlikely to be able to upgrade, you probably need to consider reverting back to Bootstrap 2.2.3, which supports IE7.

Note that if you would like to see what this message looks like, and perhaps customize its style, you can view it in any browser by temporarily deleting or commenting out the IE comment at the beginning (`<!--[if lte IE 7]>`) and at the end (`<![endif]-->`).

Setting up major structural elements

We're almost ready for page content. Right now, there's only a paragraph. Let's go ahead and get a bit more content rolling. Specifically, we'll create the following:

- A banner space with our logo and navigation
- A main content space for page content
- A footer area for copyright information and social links

We'll set this up using current HTML5 best practices with the support of major **Accessible Rich Internet Applications (ARIA)** role attributes (with roles such as banner, navigation, main, and contentinfo). If you've been following HTML5 but not closely in the past few months, note the recently added element, `<main role="main"></main>`, whose purpose is to provide a sectioning element dedicated to the main content of a page or section. For more information, see this **sitepoint** article at `http://www.sitepoint.com/html5-main-element/`.

So, consider the following comment and paragraph:

```
<!-- Add your site or application content here -->
<p>Hello world! This is HTML5 Boilerplate.</p>
```

And replace the preceding code with the following:

```
<header role="banner">
  <nav role="navigation">
  </nav>
</header>

<main role="main">
  <h1>Main Heading</h1>
  <p>Content specific to this page goes here.</p>
</main>

<footer role="contentinfo">
  <p><small>Copyright &copy; Company Name</small></p>
</footer>
```

This gives us some basic page structure and content. Let's keep rolling.

Providing a navbar markup

You'll remember that we have not brought over the precompiled CSS files from Bootstrap, nor have we yet compiled CSS from our LESS files. We'll do the latter shortly. But first, let's put at least one Bootstrap-specific element in place, that is, the navbar.

Initially, we want only Bootstrap's basic navbar (we'll add other details later). I've used the markup taken from Bootstrap's documentation and adjusted it in the following ways:

- I've added the class `navbar-static-top` since we want the navbar to be positioned at the very top, and yet scroll with the page
- I've linked the brand link to `index.html`
- I've changed the parent `div` tags to semantic HTML5 `nav` tags

The preceding adjustments lead to the following result, nested with our header element:

```
<header role="banner">
  <nav role="navigation" class="navbar navbar-static-top navbar-
    default">
  <div class="container">
    <div class="navbar-header">
      <a class="navbar-brand" href="index.html">Project name</a>
    </div>
    <ul class="nav navbar-nav">
      <li class="active"><a href="index.html">Home</a></li>
      <li><a href="#">Link</a></li>
      <li><a href="#">Link</a></li>
    </ul>
  </div>
  </nav>
</header>
```

Save your results, and open or refresh `index.html` in your browser. You'll note that we don't have much yet, as shown in the following screenshot:

We have content. Now, we desperately need our stylesheet to come to the rescue. Let's compile and link up Bootstrap's default styles.

Compiling and linking default Bootstrap CSS

We could have just brought over Bootstrap's default `bootstrap.css` file, but let's use this opportunity to take a trial run at compiling the LESS files. This will ensure we've got the fundamentals ready for doing more serious work to come.

Compiling Bootstrap CSS

If you've worked with LESS before, this will be a familiar territory. If you have not worked with LESS before, I'll help you along. However, I highly recommend that you stop and refer to the documentation at `http://lesscss.org`. Additionally, you may want to find a good basic LESS tutorial and work through it. As you'll soon see, working with LESS is powerful and fun, and the time spent learning will reward well.

For this first step, we won't be writing any LESS files, only compiling.

Navigate to `less/bootstrap.less` and open it in your editor. You'll see that this file imports all the other files from the `less` folder. When compiled, this file generates the complete `bootstrap.css` stylesheet. This is what we want for our first step.

If you've not compiled LESS files before, you'll need to download and install one of the following compilers:

- For Windows users, download and install the following compiler:
    - WinLess (a free desktop application), which can be found at `http://winless.org`

- For Mac users, download and install the following compilers:
    - The LESS app (free), which can be found at `http://incident57.com/less/`
    - CodeKit (not free), which can be found at `http://incident57.com/codekit/`

Once your chosen LESS compiler is downloaded, installed, and ready for action, the following are your steps to be performed:

1. Create a new folder named `css` in the main directory at the same level as the `fonts`, `img`, `js`, and `less` folders.

2. Use one of the following two methods to add your project's main folder (the parent folder of `css`, `fonts`, `img`, `less`, and so on) to your compiler:

   ◦ Drag-and-drop the folder into the application window

   ◦ Alternatively, navigate to the application's **File | New Project** menu to add the parent folder

3. You should see that the application loads the LESS files (and perhaps other files) into its window. Search or scan for the `less/bootstrap.less` file.

4. Right-click on `bootstrap.less`. Select **Set output path** (or your application's similar option). Navigate to the `css` folder you created earlier. The file should automatically be named `bootstrap.css`. Click on **Select**.

5. With the output path set, now click on **Compile**.

6. Check to see that `bootstrap.css` was created in the `css` folder.

> If you run into problems, check your compiler's log to ensure it was successful, then double-check your output path. In addition, you may run into a situation where your chosen compiler runs into an error because it has not been updated to stay in sync with the development of LESS. I have recently found this with another free compiler. If your compiler refuses to compile the default Bootstrap LESS files, it's an indication that the compiler needs updating.

7. Once the file is in place in the `css` folder, we only need to coordinate our file's name with the stylesheet link in our `index.html` file.

8. In `index.html`, remove the stylesheet link to `css/normalize.css`, as normalize is included in Bootstrap (`normalize.less` is the first file imported by `bootstrap.less`).

9. The remaining stylesheet link looks for the `css/main.css` file. Because we'll be customizing Bootstrap to generate our own custom stylesheet, let's leave this link as it is. In the forthcoming steps, we'll use `main.css` for the custom styles we generate.

10. For now, let's cheat by making a copy of `bootstrap.css`. In the `css` folder, create a copy of `bootstrap.css`. Name the copy as `main.css` (in the future steps, we'll overwrite this file with our customizations) as shown in the following screenshot:

11. Refresh your browser. You should now see Bootstrap 3's default navigation styles, and you'll see some typographic enhancements as shown in the following screenshot. This is Bootstrap CSS at work. Congratulations!

We now have the default Bootstrap styles in place. Now, let's complete our navbar by making it responsive. As a bonus, this will test to ensure that Bootstrap's JavaScript plugins are working as they should.

Completing the responsive navbar

To complete our navbar to take advantage of Bootstrap's responsive navbar solution, we need to add two new elements, with appropriate classes and data attributes. You'll find this documented under Bootstrap's **Components** page, under the **Navbar** tab at `http://getbootstrap.com/components/#navbar`.

We'll begin by adding the necessary additional markup as follows:

1. Search for `<div class="navbar-header">`. Inside this element, we'll add the `navbar-toggle` button, which will be used to slide the responsive navbar open and closed. The following is what you'll need (and I will include the `navbar-header` as the parent element):

```
<div class="navbar-header">
  <button type="button" class="navbar-toggle" data-
    toggle="collapse" data-target=".navbar-collapse">
    <span class="icon-bar"></span>
    <span class="icon-bar"></span>
    <span class="icon-bar"></span>
  </button>
  <a class="navbar-brand" href="index.html">Project
    name</a>
</div>
```

A few notes about the preceding code are as follows:

   ° The button includes a class of `navbar-toggle` for CSS styles.
   ° The data attributes are used by Bootstrap's collapse JavaScript plugin to indicate its desired behavior and its desired target, namely an element with the `navbar-collapse` class. This element is coming in the next step.
   ° The spans of the `icon-bar` class are used by the CSS to create the small horizontal bars in the toggle button.

2. Now to wrap the navigation items within a collapsing div, wrap `<ul class="nav navbar-nav">` with a div with the appropriate Bootstrap classes as follows:

```
<div class="navbar-collapse collapse">
  <ul class="nav navbar-nav">
    <li class="active"><a href="index.html">Home</a></li>
    <li><a href="#">Link</a></li>
    <li><a href="#">Link</a></li>
  </ul>
</div><!--/.nav-collapse -->
```

In the preceding two steps, I've divided the resulting code into two halves and all within `<div class="container">`. To double-check your work, see the full code in the sample code for this chapter.

The tag structure, class names, or data attributes may change with future versions of Bootstrap. If yours does not work as it should, be sure to check Bootstrap's own documentation. As a fallback option, you can start with the starting files provided with the sample code for this book.

Now save the file and refresh your browser. Using a modern browser (such as IE9 or a recent version of Firefox, Google Chrome, or Safari), click on and drag the edge of the browser window to make the window narrower than 980px.

If all works as it should, you should see a collapsed version of the navbar, as shown in the following screenshot, with the site name or logo and a toggle button.

This is a good sign! Now click on the toggle button, and it should slide open, as shown in the following screenshot:

Success! Congratulations!

Troubleshooting

If things are running smoothly at this point, it means that you've successfully compiled Bootstrap's CSS from LESS, and you've also successfully included Bootstrap's JavaScript plugins.

If things are not running smoothly, you should double-check the following things:

- Is your markup properly structured? Any unclosed, incomplete, or malformed tags, classes, and so on present?
- Did you successfully compile Bootstrap's LESS to CSS? And did the resulting CSS file wind up in the correct folder under the proper name?
- Is the CSS link in the head of `index.html` updated as it should be?
- Have you successfully included Bootstrap's JavaScript plugins?

You might find it helpful to do the following:

1. Work back through the preceding steps, double-checking things along the way.
2. Validate your HTML to ensure it's well formed.
3. Compare the completed version of the exercise files with your own.
4. Refer to the Bootstrap documentation for new updates to the relevant tag structures and attributes.
5. Place your code in a snippet at `http://jsfiddle.net/` or `http://www.codepen.com/`, and share it with the good folks at `http://stackoverflow.com/` for help.

When we have so many moving parts to work with, things do happen. And these are some of our best survival methods!

Now, assuming things are working, let's move on to take care of one more potential problem. We intend to support Internet Explorer 8 in our designs. To do this, we need to help this older browser out a little.

Adding support for Internet Explorer 8

To support Internet Explorer 8, we need to add a bit of JavaScript that equips the browser to respond to media queries. This is the `respond.js` polyfill by Scott Jehl.

Bootstrap's own documentation recommends this step for IE8 compatibility. You'll find it referenced briefly in the Bootstrap 3 documentation at `http://getbootstrap.com/getting-started/#browsers`.

You'll also find `respond.js` linked in the example HTML templates found in the `bootstrap-master` download under the `examples` folder, which is found in the **docs** folder. There you'll see `respond.js` linked in the head of the document within an IE conditional comment that limits its use to IE browsers lower than IE9. The HTML5 shiv is also included as follows:

```
<!--[if lt IE 9]>
  <script src="../../assets/js/html5shiv.js"></script>
  <script src="../../assets/js/respond.min.js"></script>
<![endif]-->
```

Because we have already included the HTML5 shiv with Modernizr, we can leave that out here. In addition, Andy Clarke has recommended an improved conditional comment that excludes IE mobile browsers to ensure that we do not unnecessarily feed the script to Windows mobile devices that don't need it. See his repository, **320andup**, at `https://github.com/malarkey/320andup/`.

Clarke's recommended code works as follows:

```
<!--[if (lt IE 9) & (!IEMobile)]>
...
<![endif]-->
```

Armed with these starting points, we're ready to implement it in our site template files as follows:

1. Navigate to `https://github.com/scottjehl/Respond` (you may also search `respond.js` and find the GitHub link). If you'd like, take a few minutes to scroll down the page and read the documentation to learn more about how it works.

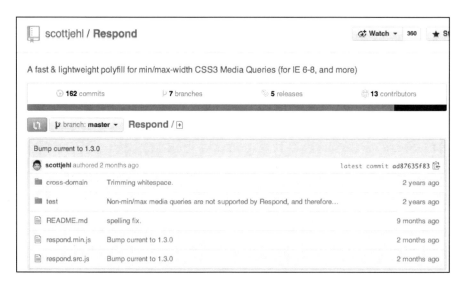

2. Now to get the file and download the ZIP repository.

3. Extract the directory, and find the minified version of the file named as `respond.min.js`.

4. Copy the file to your project files in the `js/vendor` directory, right alongside the scripts for jQuery and Modernizr.

5. Then, add the following lines of code to load the `respond.js` file, which is wrapped in the targeted IE conditional comment. We'll do this is in the head of `index.html`, directly beneath the line loading Modernizr.

```
<!-- Modernizr -->
<script src="js/vendor/modernizr-2.6.2.min.js"></script>
<!-- Respond.js for IE 8 or less only -->
<!--[if (lt IE 9) & (!IEMobile)]>
   <script src="js/vendor/respond.min.js"></script>
<![endif]-->
```

6. That's it! We've successfully provided IE8 with what it needs so that it responds, as it should, to our mobile-first responsive websites.

 If you want to test this and do not have IE8 available, you might use an online service such as Browsershots that is available at `http://browsershots.org` (free) or BrowserStack that is available at `http://www.browserstack.com` (premium with free trial).

Our site template is almost complete. Let's pause to take stock before moving on.

Summary

If you've made it this far, you have everything you need ready to do some serious work. Taking stock of our progress, we have the following:

- A solid HTML5 markup structure with many current best practices baked in
- A standard Bootstrap stylesheet linked up
- JavaScript linked up and working
- A responsive navbar
- Perhaps the most important, we have our LESS compiler ready and working

 This may be a good point to save a copy of these files so that they're ready for other future projects.

Now it's time to have some fun. In the next chapter, we'll take Bootstrap for a spin, creating a beautiful portfolio site.

Bootstrappin' Your Portfolio

2

Let's imagine we're ready for a fresh design of our online portfolio. As always, time is scarce. We need to be efficient, but the portfolio has to look great. And of course, it has to be responsive. It should work across devices of various form factors, since this is a key selling point for our prospective clients. This project will enable us to leverage a number of Bootstrap's built-in features, even as we customize Bootstrap to suit our needs.

What we'll build

We've thrown together a couple of home page mock-ups. Though we have in mind what we want for large screens, we've begun with a handheld screen size to force ourselves to focus on the essentials.

You'll notice the following features:

- A collapsed responsive navbar with logo
- A sliding carousel with four images of featured portfolio items
- A single-column layout with three blocks of content, each with a heading, short paragraph, and a nice big button with an invitation to read further
- A footer with social media links

Here is the design mockup as shown in the following screenshot:

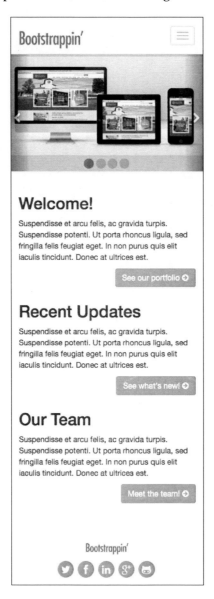

Altogether, this should provide a good introduction to our work. The carousel is tall enough to give a good amount of visual space to our portfolio images. It is not difficult to navigate quickly to the content below, where a user can efficiently scan key options for taking a next step inside. By presenting key links as nice big buttons, we will establish helpful visual hierarchy for the key action items, and we will ensure that visitors do not have problems because of fat fingers.

For ease of maintenance, we've elected to have only two major breakpoints in this design. We'll use the single-column layout for screen sizes narrower than 768px. Then, we'll shift to a three-column layout:

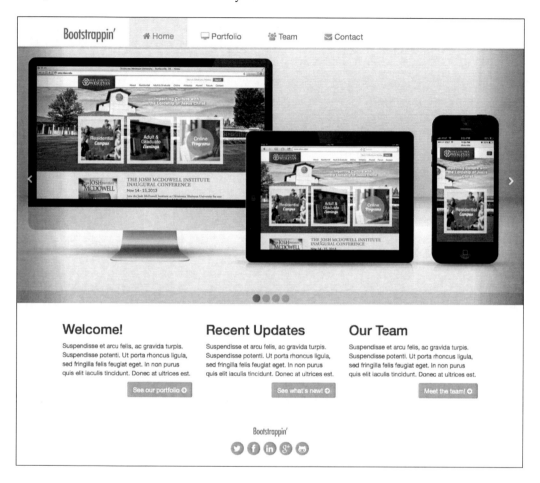

You'll note the following features in the mock-up for tablets and higher versions:

- A navigation bar at the top, which is enhanced with icons
- A widescreen version of the home page carousel, with images stretching to fill the full width of the browser
- A three-column layout for our textual content blocks
- A footer with content at the center

The color scheme is fairly simple: shades of gray, plus a golden-green color for links and highlights.

With these design goals in mind, we'll proceed to get our content in place.

Surveying the exercise files

Let's survey the beginning files for this exercise, which you will find in the folder `02_Code_BEGIN`. You'll see files similar to the template we set up in *Chapter 1, Getting Started with Bootstrap*.

There are a few new additions:

- The `less` folder has a slightly modified organization scheme. We'll return to this later in the project. First, let's attend to the content elements.

- The `img` folder now contains five images:
  - One logo image, named `logo.png`
  - Four portfolio item images

- The `index.html` file has the following new touches:
  - Navbar items have been updated to reflect our new site architecture
  - We also have the essential markup in place for the images, content blocks, a logo in the footer, and social links

Other than the navbar, which we set up in *Chapter 1, Getting Started with Bootstrap*, no Bootstrap classes have been added to style the carousel, columns, or icons yet. You can view the results in your browser.

You'll see the navbar, followed by the portfolio images:

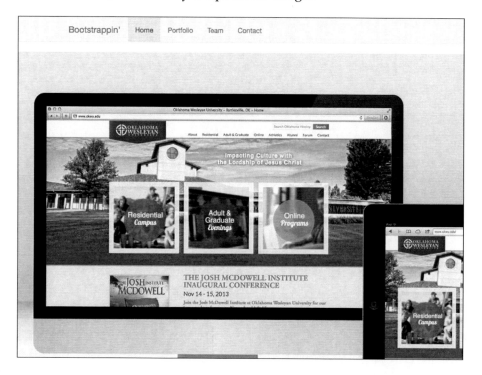

The blocks of text and the footer with a list of social links follows after the images.

Welcome!

Suspendisse et arcu felis, ac gravida turpis. Suspendisse potenti. Ut porta rhoncus ligula, sed fringilla felis feugiat eget. In non purus quis elit iaculis tincidunt. Donec at ultrices est.

See our portfolio

Recent Updates

Suspendisse et arcu felis, ac gravida turpis. Suspendisse potenti. Ut porta rhoncus ligula, sed fringilla felis feugiat eget. In non purus quis elit iaculis tincidunt. Donec at ultrices est.

See what's new!

Our Team

Suspendisse et arcu felis, ac gravida turpis. Suspendisse potenti. Ut porta rhoncus ligula, sed fringilla felis feugiat eget. In non purus quis elit iaculis tincidunt. Donec at ultrices est.

Meet the team!

Bootstrappin'

- Twitter
- Facebook
- LinkedIn
- Google+
- GitHub

It's not much to speak of yet. Let the transformation begin.

We'll begin by applying the Bootstrap classes, allowing us to quickly and efficiently establish the fundamentals for our interface elements using Bootstrap's default CSS styles and JavaScript behaviors.

Marking up the carousel

Let's get started with our carousel, which will rotate between four featured images from our portfolio.

Bootstrap's carousel markup structure can be found in its documentation pages at the following URL:

```
http://getbootstrap.com/javascript/#carousel
```

Following the pattern used in the example, we'll begin with this structure to set up the fundamental element. This will contain all parts of the carousel, followed by the progress indicators:

```html
<div id="homepage-feature" class="carousel slide">
  <ol class="carousel-indicators">
    <li data-target="#homepage-feature" data-slide-to="0"
      class="active"></li>
    <li data-target="#homepage-feature" data-slide-to="1"></li>
    <li data-target="#homepage-feature" data-slide-to="2"></li>
    <li data-target="#homepage-feature" data-slide-to="3"></li>
  </ol>
```

Note that I've used a `div` tag with an ID (`id="homepage-feature"`) to establish the fundamental context of `carousel`. The `carousel` class applies the Bootstrap's carousel CSS to the carousel elements, adding appropriate styles to the carousel indicators, the carousel items, and the next and previous controls.

The `homepage-feature` ID must be used in the `data-target` attributes of the progress indicators. This signals the JavaScript plugin to update the indicator for the active carousel item with the `active` class. We've provided that class for the first indicator to get things started. From there, the JavaScript takes over. It removes the class, and adds it to the appropriate indicator as the carousel cycles.

Also, note that the `data-slide-to` values begin counting from `0`. This is the standard behavior for JavaScript and other programming languages. Just remember: start counting at zero, not one.

After the indicators, the element of the class `carousel-inner` follows. This serves as the wrapper to contain all of the carousel items—in this case, our images.

The carousel items come within `carousel-inner`. They are a group of `div` tags, each with `class="item"`. Modify the first item to have both the classes item and active, to make it visible from the outset.

Thus, the markup structure works as follows:

```html
<!-- Wrapper for slides -->
<div class="carousel-inner">
  <div class="item active">
    <img src="img/okwu-athletics.jpg" alt="OKWU Athletics Homepage">
  </div>
  <div class="item">
    <img src="img/okwu.jpg" alt="OKWU.edu Homepage">
  </div>
  <div class="item">
    <img src="img/bso.jpg" alt="Bartlesville Symphony Homepage">
  </div>
  <div class="item">
    <img src="img/alittlecode.jpg" alt="aLittleCode.com Homepage">
  </div>
</div><!-- /.carousel-inner -->
```

After the carousel items, we need to add the carousel-controls. These will provide the next and previous buttons at the left and right edges of the carousel. You'll see that these have classes that correspond to icons from the included **Glyphicon** font icons. After the controls, we'll close up our entire markup structure with the closing `div` tag.

```html
<!-- Controls -->
  <a class="left carousel-control" href="#homepage-feature" data-slide="prev">
    <span class="glyphicon glyphicon-chevron-left"></span>
  </a>
  <a class="right carousel-control" href="#homepage-feature"
    data-slide="next">
  <span class="glyphicon glyphicon-chevron-right"></span>
  </a>
</div><!-- /#homepage-feature.carousel -->
```

The carousel-controls need to have the ID of the fundamental carousel element (#homepage-feature) for their href value.

Once this code is in place, save your work and refresh your browser. Bootstrap's styles and JavaScript should start working. Your images should now work as a sliding carousel!

By default, the carousel will slide every 5 seconds. Let's set the interval to 8 seconds, to give our users time to appreciate the full beauty of our work:

1. Open `js/main.js`.

2. Add the following lines. We'll begin with the jQuery method of checking to ensure page elements are ready, and then initialize the carousel with an interval of 8000 milliseconds.

```
$( document ).ready(function() {
  $('.carousel').carousel({
    interval: 8000
  });
});
```

3. Save and refresh. You will see that the interval has increased to 8 seconds.

For this and other options, see the Bootstrap carousel documentation at `http://getbootstrap.com/javascript/#carousel`.

We'll return to customize the styling of the carousel, its indicators, and its icons later in the chapter. First, let's continue leveraging the power of Bootstrap's default styles and set up a responsive grid for the content below the carousel.

Creating responsive columns

We have three blocks of text, each with a heading, a short paragraph, and a link. In screen sizes of approximately tablet width or more, we would like this content to be laid out in three columns. In narrower screen widths, the content will organize itself in one full-width column.

Take a moment to visit and read the documentation for Bootstrap's mobile-first responsive grid. You can find it at `http://getbootstrap.com/css/#grid`.

In short, the grid is based on a twelve-column system. The basic class structure allows us to use a class of `col-12` for full-width, `col-6` for half-width, `col-4` for one-third width, and so on.

With Bootstrap 3, thanks to the creative use of media queries, Bootstrap's grid can be very adept. Recall that we want our welcome message to have a single-column layout up to tablet-sized screens, and then adapt a three-column layout at approximately 768px. Conveniently, Bootstrap has a built-in breakpoint at 768px, which is the default value of its `@screen-sm-min` variable. Above 768px is the medium range beginning at 992px, corresponding to a `@screen-md-min` variable, then the large screen, beginning at 1200px and up. I'll refer to these as Bootstrap's small, medium, and large breakpoints.

With the small breakpoint there is a special column class that uses the formulation `col-sm-`. Because we want three columns after the small breakpoint, we'll use `class="col-sm-4"`. Below the small breakpoint, the elements will remain full-width. Above it, they will shift to 1/3 width and line up side by side. The full structure is given here, with paragraph contents abbreviated for clarity:

```
<div class="container">
  <div class="row">
    <div class="col-sm-4">
    <h2>Welcome!</h2>
    <p>Suspendisse et arcu felis ...</p>
    <p><a href="#">See our portfolio</a></p>
  </div>
  <div class="col-sm-4">
    <h2>Recent Updates</h2>
    <p>Suspendisse et arcu felis ...</p>
    <p><a href="#">See what's new!</a></p>
  </div>
  <div class="col-sm-4">
    <h2>Our Team</h2>
    <p>Suspendisse et arcu felis ...</p>
    <p><a href="#">Meet the team!</a></p>
  </div>
  </div><!-- /.row -->
</div><!-- /.container -->
```

If you're unfamiliar with the `container` and `row` classes, here is what they do:

- The `container` class constrains the width of the content and keeps it centered within the page
- The `row` class provides the wrapper for our columns, allowing extra left and right margin for the column gutters
- Both the `container` class and the `row` class are `clearfixed`, so that they contain floating elements and clear any previous floating elements

Now, save and refresh. With your browser width above 768px, you should see the following three-column layout take shape:

Resize your browser window below 768px, and you'll see it revert to a single column.

With our responsive grid in place, let's turn those links into clearly visible calls to action by utilizing Bootstrap's button styles.

Turning links into buttons

Turning our key content links into visually effective buttons is straightforward. The key classes we'll employ are as follows:

- The `btn` class will style a link as a button

- The `btn-primary` class will assign a button the color of our primary brand color

- The `pull-right` class will float the link to the right, moving it into wider space to make it a more appealing target

Add these classes to the link at the end of each of our three content blocks:

```
<p><a class="btn btn-primary pull-right" href="#">See our portfolio</a></p>
```

Save and refresh. You should see the following result:

We've made great progress. Our key elements are taking shape.

With our fundamental markup structure in place, we can start working on the finer details. Getting there will require some custom CSS. We're going to approach this by leveraging the power of Bootstrap's LESS files. If you're new to LESS, no worries! I'll walk you through it step by step.

Understanding the power of LESS

In the following sections, we will be organizing, editing, customizing, and creating LESS files in order to generate the desired CSS for our designs.

If you are unfamiliar with LESS and would like to learn more about it, I would recommend the following resources:

- LESS documentation at `http://lesscss.org/#docs`.
- *A Comprehensive Introduction to LESS* from the Sitepoint website, `http://www.sitepoint.com/a-comprehensive-introduction-to-less/`

In a nutshell, we may say that generating CSS using the LESS preprocessor is an exciting and freeing experience. The key benefits of working with LESS are discussed in the following sections.

Nested rules

Nested rules greatly enhance the efficiency of composing styles. For example, writing selectors in CSS can be highly repetitive:

```
.navbar-nav { ... }
.navbar-nav > li { ... }
.navbar-nav > li > a { ... }
.navbar-nav > li > a:hover,
.navbar-nav > li > a:focus { ... }
```

This same set of selectors and their styles can be written much more easily in LESS, by means of a simple nesting pattern:

```
.navbar-nav { ...
  > li { ...
    > a { ...
      &:hover,
      &:focus { ... }
    }
  }
}
```

Once compiled, these rules come out as standard CSS. But, the nesting pattern makes the LESS styles much easier to write and maintain.

Variables

Variables make it possible to specify a value once (or revise it), and then use it automatically (or updated) throughout your entire stylesheet. For example, we may use color variables, such as the following:

```
@off-white:    #e5e5e5;
@brand-primary:  #890000;
```

When we update the value of these variables, we can automatically update colors throughout the site. This is because we have used the variables throughout our LESS files in rules, such as the following:

```
a {
  color: @brand-primary;
```

```
}
.navbar {
  background-color: @brand-primary;
  > li > a {
  color: @off-white;
  }
}
```

Mixins

Mixins make it possible to generate an entire set of rules using concise and easy-to-manage formulations. For example, we can simplify the task of applying the desired border-box properties to elements. In CSS, we would have to add three lines to each element to cover all the browsers and their vendor prefixes, requiring considerable mental load to remember which prefixes are needed:

```
.box {
  -webkit-box-sizing: border-box;
    -moz-box-sizing: border-box;
         box-sizing: border-box;
}
```

In LESS, we can write one rule as a mixin, with an @boxmodel parameter for specifying our desired box model:

```
.box-sizing(@boxmodel) {
  -webkit-box-sizing: @boxmodel;
    -moz-box-sizing: @boxmodel;
         box-sizing: @boxmodel;
}
```

Then, we can use this mixin wherever needed:

```
.box {
  .box-sizing(border-box);
}
.another-element {
  .box-sizing(border-box);
}
```

When compiled, each element will get its essential three lines of CSS.

Operations

Operations make it possible to do math, including math with variables. We can start with one color, and then lighten or darken it to get variations as follows:

```
a:hover { darken(@link-color, 15%); }
```

We can also calculate padding values to fit our available navbar height. Thus, the following lines from Bootstrap's `navbar.less` file set the nav item padding values to the amount of vertical space we have left after subtracting the line height. Then, we take that remaining value and divide by two, to share it evenly between the top and bottom padding:

```
.navbar > li > a {
  padding-top: ((@navbar-height - @line-height-computed) / 2);
  padding-bottom: ((@navbar-height - @line-height-computed) / 2);
}
```

Importing files

The LESS compiling process makes it possible to import and combine multiple files into a single, unified CSS file. We can specify the order of import, organizing the resulting stylesheet precisely as needed for our desired cascade.

Thus, Bootstrap's import file, `bootstrap.css`, begins with imports for essential variables and mixins. Then, it imports a LESS version of `normalize.css` (in place of a CSS reset), followed by basic styles for print media. Then, it moves to basic global styles (`scaffolding.less`), typographic fundamentals, and more specific details. Thus, the first several lines of the current `bootstrap.less` file are given as follows:

```
// Core variables and mixins
@import "variables.less";
@import "mixins.less";

// Reset
@import "normalize.less";
@import "print.less";

// Core CSS
@import "scaffolding.less";
@import "type.less";
```

The resulting CSS file will be a single, unified whole, with styles cascading down from the general to the specific, just as they should.

The modular file organization

Because of the ability to import distinct files into a unified whole, we may easily organize our styles in coherent groupings and maintain them in distinct files. This is why Bootstrap comes with so many LESS files—one dedicated to navbar styles, another to buttons, another for alerts, one for carousel styles, and so on—all imported using the `bootstrap.less` file.

For these reasons and others, LESS and its cousin preprocessors are more than a fad. They have become part of the standard practice for professional web development. Most developers agree that they point to the future of CSS.

Customizing Bootstrap's LESS according to our needs

As we work with Bootstrap's LESS files, we'll exert considerable control over them, including the following:

- Organizing our `less` folder to give us flexibility and freedom to accomplish what we need, while making future maintenance easier

- Customizing several LESS files provided by Bootstrap

- Creating a few custom LESS files of our own

- Incorporating a larger set of font-based icons in our site assets, doubling the number of available icons, and providing the icons that we need for our social media links

In other words, we'll be doing more than merely learning and applying Bootstrap's conventions. We'll be bending them to our will.

In this chapter's exercise files, open the `less` directory. Inside, you should see the following structure:

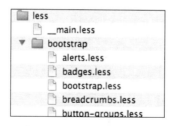

To prepare for what's ahead, I've given you a head start by adding a new layer of organization. All of Bootstrap's `less` files are now organized under the `bootstrap` subdirectory.

The file `__main.less` is a modified copy of `bootstrap.less`. This file imports all other files, and it is used in the compiling process to create one unified stylesheet from all of our imported LESS files. If you open `__main.less`, you'll see that at present it is very much like `bootstrap.less`, except that the import paths are updated to reach into the `Bootstrap` folder.

```
// Core variables and mixins
@import "bootstrap/variables.less";
@import "bootstrap/mixins.less";
```

Why go through this trouble? Because we'll soon be creating custom files of our own. When we do that, we can leave the `Bootstrap` folder and its files intact as they are, while making adjustments in the custom files that we will create.

You may wonder if there is a good reason for the two underscores at the beginning of this file name. In fact there are four good reasons:

- When files are sorted alphabetically in the file browser, the underscore helps this file filter to the top.
- This will not be our only custom file. If we place a single underscore at the front of our other custom files, the double underscore will ensure that this key file finds its way to the top of the heap.
- By employing this pattern, we gain advantages when scanning or searching for our custom files. Visually the underscores stand out. When typing a search, the opening underscore will immediately bring up all of our custom files.
- When we have multiple files open for editing, the underscored version of a file name will again provide a useful visual indicator for our custom files.

Armed with this strategy, let us begin the customization! We'll begin by customizing Bootstrap's variables and adding a few new variables of our own.

Customizing variables

Let's move forward in the way we've begun. We'll create a copy of Bootstrap's variables file and customize it to our needs.

1. Find Bootstrap's `variables.less` file in the `less/bootstrap` folder, and open it in your editor.

2. Scanning through the lines of this file, you'll see variables used to set the CSS values for everything from basic colors to the body background, font-families, navbar height and background, and so on. It's beautiful to behold. It's even more fun to meddle with. Before we meddle, let's create our own copy of this file, allowing us to leave Bootstrap's default variables intact in case we ever want to revert back to them.

3. Save a copy of this file outside of the `bootstrap` folder in the main `less` directory, right beside `__main.less`. To mark this file as our own, add an underscore at the beginning, so that its name becomes `_variables.less`.

You should now have the following file scheme:

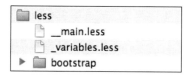

Next, let's implement our new color scheme.

1. In the topmost section of our new `_variables.less` file, you'll see the default Bootstrap variables for grays and brand colors. Note that the default set of grays is calculated in percentages of black, using the LESS `lighten` function:

        @gray-darker: lighten(#000, 13.5%); // #222
        @gray-dark

2. We have the specific values that we're after. So, let's simply substitute our desired values. (Feel free to do the math if you prefer!) Then, we'll add an additional two variables to encompass the full range that we need.

3. The result is as follows:

        @gray-darker: #222;
        @gray-dark: #454545;
        @gray: #777;
        @gray-light: #aeaeae;
        @gray-lighter: #ccc;
        @gray-lightest: #ededed;
        @off-white: #fafafa;

Next, we'll update the `@brand-primary` variable under `Brand colors`. We'll adjust this to our gold hue:

```
// Brand colors
// ------------------------
@brand-primary:            #c1ba62;
```

To see the results, we'll need to import our new variables and compile the updated CSS.

Importing our new variables

We need to update `__main.less` to import our new `_variables.less` file.

1. In `__main.less`, find the line that imports the file `bootstrap/variables.less`. This is the first import, on line 12 of the file.

2. Update this line, so that it grabs our new `_variables.less` file instead. Remove `bootstrap/` from the path, and adjust the file name with the leading underscore.

    ```
    @import "_variables.less";
    ```

3. Now, to compile to CSS—if you've not yet done it, add this new project to your compiler of choice.

     Your compiler may need you to refresh its view of the files, so that it finds the new `_variables.less` file and adds it to the project. (CodeKit requires this.)

4. Select the file `__main.less` to compile. (If given the option, go ahead and minify and/or compress it while you're at it.)

5. Set the output path to `css/main.css`. (Recall that this is the file linked to `index.html` as its stylesheet.)

     If your compiler makes it difficult to strip out the underscores for the compiled filename, simply add the underscores to the stylesheet link in the head of `index.html`.

6. Compile! Then refresh `index.html` in your browser.

If this is successful, the most noticeable change will be in the link color and buttons with the `btn-primary` class, which will both take the new `@brand-primary` color.

Editing navbar variables

Now, let's edit the variables that set the navbar height, colors, and hover effects.

1. In `_variables.less`, search for these variables and update them with the following values. These will expand the navbar height, employ our brand color for links, and make use of our other color variables where relevant.

    ```
    @navbar-height:                     64px;
    @navbar-margin-bottom:              0;
    ...
    navbar-default-color:               @gray;
    @navbar-default-bg:                 #fff;
    @@navbar-default-border:             @gray-light;
    ...
    // Navbar links
    @navbar-default-link-color:              @navbar-default-color;
    @navbar-default-link-hover-color:        @link-hover-color;
    @navbar-default-link-hover-bg:           @off-white;
    @navbar-default-link-active-color:       @link-hover-color;
    @navbar-default-link-active-bg:          @gray-lightest;
    @navbar-default-link-disabled-color      @gray-lighter;
    @navbar-default-link-disabled-bg:        transparent;
    ```

2. Save your changes, compile, and refresh.

You should see the following new features in your navbar:

*   It should grow 14px taller
*   Its background color should turn white
*   It should have a slightly darker bottom border
*   Nav item backgrounds should darken slightly on hover
*   The active nav item background should be a tad darker
*   Link text should turn our brand-primary color on hover and when active, as shown in the following screenshot:

Now, let's put our logo image in place.

Adding the logo image

Find the `logo.png` file in the `img` folder. You may notice that its dimensions are large, 900px wide. In our final design, it will be only 120px wide. Because the pixels will be compressed into a smaller space, this is a relatively easy way to ensure that the image will look good in all devices, including retina displays. Meanwhile, the file size of the image, which has already been optimized for the Web, is only 19 KB.

So, let's put it in place and constrain its width.

1. Open `index.html` in your editor.

2. Search for this line within the navbar markup:

   ```
   <a class="navbar-brand" href="index.html">Bootstrappin'</a>
   ```

3. Replace `Bootstrappin'` with this image tag, including its `alt` and `width` attributes.

   ```
   <img src="img/logo.png" alt="Bootstrappin'" width="120">
   ```

    Be sure to include the `width` attribute, setting its width to 120px. Otherwise, it will appear *very* large on the page.

4. Save `index.html` and refresh your browser. You should see the logo in place.

You may notice that the navbar height has expanded, and that its bottom edge no longer lines up with the bottom edge of the active nav item. This is due to the default padding placed around `navbar-brand`. We need to adjust the appropriate padding values. We can do that in a few quick steps.

1. Open the file `bootstrap/navbar.less` in your editor.

2. Search for the selector and its curly brace: `.navbar-brand {`.

3. At around line 150, you should find the following lines:

   ```
   .navbar-brand {
     float: left;
     padding: @navbar-padding-vertical @navbar-padding-
       horizontal;
   ```

   The padding values are what we're after.

4. As we're now in the mode of customizing this file, let's save it as our own custom file and name it `_navbar.less`.

5. Save it in your `less` folder, alongside `__main.less` and `_variables.less`.

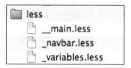

6. We're going to comment out the original values, and then add our own custom padding values. To do this in LESS, simply add two slashes in front of the line, as follows:

```
// padding: @navbar-padding-vertical @navbar-padding-
   horizontal;
padding: 22px 30px 0 15px;
```

When compiled, the line that's commented out in this manner will not be compiled to CSS.

7. To try this, make the previous change in your `_navbar.less` file and save it.

8. Then, in `__main.less`, find and comment out the import line for Bootstrap's `navbar.less` file. Then, add an import for the new `_navbar.less` file just after it.

```
// @import "bootstrap/navbar.less";
@import "_navbar.less";
```

9. Save the file. Make sure that `_navbar.less` is added to your project in your compiler, and then compile `__main.less` to `css/main.css`.

    Refresh the browser. You should see the bottom edge of your navbar line back up with the bottom edge of the active link. (You should also see some additional padding between the logo and the **Home** link.)

10. Now, open `main.css` in your editor and search for the selector `.navbar {`.

    Since I've minified my CSS output, mine looks like this: `.navbar-brand{float:left;padding:22px 30px 0 15px;`.

> There is no trace of the line we commented out, as it was not compiled from LESS to CSS!

The powers of LESS continue to impress. Observe what we've done here:

- We've left the original `bootstrap/navbar.less` file just as it was in its original state, so that we can revert back to it if needed

- We've entirely replaced it for now with our own custom version of the file, and we've indicated where this happens by leaving a comment trail in `__main.less`

- We've also left a comment trail for ourselves in `_navbar.less`, so that we can see where we've been modifying rules

- But because we've used JavaScript-style single-line comments, we've done all of this *without* adding these comments to the final compiled CSS

In other words, we can leave ourselves a rich trail of fallback files and helpful comments—all with no code bloat. Nice bonus.

Adjusting nav item padding

Now, let's adjust our nav items so that the text of our links shares the same baseline as our logo.

In `_navbar.less`, find the selector `.navbar-nav`. It is the parent `ul` of our navbar items. Within this set of rules, you'll find nested media queries. (See the documentation on nested media queries at `http://lesscss.org`.) The relevant lines are given as follows:

```
// Uncollapse the nav
  @media (min-width: @grid-float-breakpoint) {
    float: left;
    margin: 0;
    > li {
      float: left;
      > a {
        padding-top: ((@navbar-height - @line-height-computed)
          / 2);
        padding-bottom: ((@navbar-height - @line-height-computed)
          / 2);
      }
    }
  }
```

The variable `@grid-float-breakpoint` specifies the point at which the navbar expands to its full width or collapses to create the mobile-app-style responsive navigation. (You'll find this variable defined in `_variables.less`.)

At present, the `padding-top` and `padding-bottom` values are calculated to keep the text in the vertical center of the navbar. We want to increase the top padding and decrease the bottom padding. While we're at it, let's increase the horizontal padding on these nav items, and nudge the font size up a bit. I'll leave a trail by commenting out the original lines with single-line comments, and then adding my own new lines:

```
> a {
  // padding-top: ((@navbar-height - @line-height-computed) / 2);
  // padding-bottom: ((@navbar-height - @line-height-computed) / 2);
  padding: 30px 30px 14px;
  font-size: 18px;
```

Save, compile, and refresh to obtain the following result:

Feeling the power yet?

Now, let's add icon powers.

Adding icons

It's time to add icons to our navigation. We'll begin by employing the Glyphicons that come with Bootstrap. Then, we'll shift to the larger library of icons offered by **Font Awesome**.

 Take a moment to review the relevant Bootstrap documentation at: `http://getbootstrap.com/components/#glyphicons`.

You'll see the set of icons available and the markup convention for using these in your HTML using span tags and glyphicon classes. We'll start by adding a home icon to our **Home** nav item:

1. Add the **Glyphicon Home** icon to the **Home** nav item by placing a span tag with appropriate classes within the nav item link and before the text:
   ```
   <li class="active">
     <a href="index.html">
       <span class="glyphicon glyphicon-home"></span> Home
     </a>
   </li>
   ```

I've added a space after the span tag to provide a bit of space between the icon and the text Home.

2. Save this and refresh your browser. If all goes well, you should see your icon appear!

3. If your icon does not appear, check the following things:

   ° Are the Glyphicon fonts in the fonts folder?

   ° Is the `@icon-font-path` variable set properly in your `_variables.less` file? The `@icon-font-path:"../fonts/";` path is working for me.

4. Assuming that all is working, let's press on and add icons to each of the other nav items. Here are the remaining span elements and classes I'll use, in this order, for **Portfolio**, **Team**, and **Contact**.

   ```
   <span class="glyphicon glyphicon-picture"></span>
   <span class="glyphicon glyphicon-user"></span>
   <span class="glyphicon glyphicon-envelope"></span>
   ```

5. Save and refresh. You should get the following result for all computer screen sizes:

6. And, in the collapsed responsive navigation:

Not too bad.

Of course, our icons don't exactly match the icons from the mock-up. Here is what the mock-up called for:

The free version of Glyphicons provided with Bootstrap does not include icons for a computer monitor or a group of people. As we look through the available Glyphicons, we'll also find there are no icons for our social media links in the footer.

Fortunately, we have other icon options available. Let's consider one of them.

Adding Font Awesome icons

Font Awesome is a font icon set that offers 361 icons at the time of writing this book—twice as many as available in the current Bootstrap version of Glyphicons. Font Awesome icons are free, open source, and built to play nice with Bootstrap. You can see the Font Awesome home page at:

`http://fortawesome.github.io/Font-Awesome/`

Let's fold Font Awesome into our workflow.

1. Navigate to the Font Awesome home page, at `http://fortawesome.github.io/Font-Awesome/`, and click on the large **Download** button.

2. Extract the downloaded archive and look inside. You'll find the following folder structure:

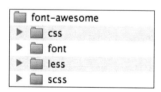

3. Inside the `font` folder, you'll find the Font Awesome icon font files.

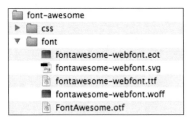

4. Copy all of these files and paste them into your project's `fonts` folder, alongside the Glyphicons font files.

5. Now, we want to copy the Font Awesome `less` files to our project's `less` directory. Create a new subdirectory named font-awesome, and copy the Font Awesome `less` files into it.

6. Next, we will import the `font-awesome.less` file into our `__main.less` file, so that it will be compiled into our stylesheet. I'll add the import line to `__main.less` just under the Glyphicon import:

```
@import "bootstrap/glyphicons.less";
@import "font-awesome/font-awesome.less";
```

7. The Font Awesome `less` files include a variable specifying the path to the Font Awesome web fonts. We need to check to make sure that this variable matches our folder structure. Open the Font Awesome variables file `font-awesome/variables.less`. Ensure that the `@fa-font-path` variable is set to `../fonts` as follows:

```
@fa-font-path:     "../fonts";
```

 This path is relative to the compiled CSS file, which is in our `css` directory.

8. Save and compile to CSS.

9. Now, in `index.html`, let's update the icon for the **Team** navbar item to use the Font Awesome icon named `fa-group`. We also need the standalone `fa` class. In addition, let's add our own generic `icon` class:

```
<span class="icon fa fa-group"></span> Team
```

10. Save this change to `index.html`, and refresh your browser.

If all works as it should, you should see the following result:

 If you see a strange symbol — or nothing — that's a sign that the web fonts are not coming through. Double-check that your icon classes are correct (including the `fa` class), your Font Awesome web font files are in your `fonts` directory, and the path is set correctly in `font-awesome/variables.less`.

Congratulations — you've more than doubled your available icons!

At this point, we can choose to keep Glyphicons in the mix, or we can unhook them. In order to reduce code bloat, I'll remove Glyphicons and shift entirely to Font Awesome. This requires only two quick steps:

1. Comment out the Glyphicons import line from `__main.less`.

```
// @import "bootstrap/glyphicons.less";
@import "font-awesome/font-awesome.less";
```

2. Update your icon markup in `index.html` to make use of the desired Font Awesome icons.

The Font Awesome icon page `http://fortawesome.github.io/Font-Awesome/icons/` allows you to scan your options. Our mock-up calls for these icons in the navbar:

```
<span class="icon fa fa-home"></span> Home
<span class="icon fa fa-desktop"></span> Portfolio
<span class="icon fa fa-group"></span> Team
<span class="icon fa fa-envelope"></span> Contact
```

With this result:

Adjusting the navbar icon color

You might note that the icons appear visually heavier than their adjacent text. The color is the same, but the icons carry greater visual weight. Let's adjust the icons to a lighter and less overpowering shade.

1. Open `_navbar.less` in your editor.

2. Search to find the selector `.navbar-default`. We have used this class in our navbar markup to apply default styles. You should find it under the commented section for `// Alternate navbars`.

3. Within this nested set of rules, find the selector `.navbar-nav` and the `> li >` selector nested beneath it. This is where we want to adjust our icon colors.

4. Under the statement defining nav item link colors, we'll nest a rule to make our icons a lighter shade, using our variable `@gray-light`, as follows:

```
.navbar-nav {
  > li > a {
    color: @navbar-default-link-color;

    .icon { // added rule set
      color: @gray-light;
    }
```

 The generic class icon proves to be a handy way to select all of our icons.

 I've begun adding a comment `// added` to help me easily search or scan to identify code that I've added into the mix.

5. Now, we need to specify that these icons should still share the same hover and active color—the `@brand-primary` color. This requires adding our icons to the selector groups just below the lines we've added. Under the `&:hover`, `&:focus` pseudo-selectors, I've added two selectors to specifically target the icons:

```
&:hover,
&:focus,
&:hover .icon, // added selector
&:focus .icon { // added selector
  color: @navbar-default-link-hover-color;
  background-color: @navbar-default-link-hover-bg;
}
```

I've targeted the icons for active links in the following code snippet:

```
> .active > a {
  &,
  &:hover,
  &:focus,
  .icon, // added selector
  &:hover .icon, // added selector
  &:focus .icon { // added selector
    color: @navbar-default-link-active-color;
    background-color: @navbar-default-link-active-bg;
  }
}
```

6. Once you've worked these in, save the file, compile to CSS, and refresh your browser. You should see the icons take a lighter shade of gray by default, and yet retain the default link color for active and hovered states.

This completes our nav—or *almost* completes it. We've inadvertently created a small problem that we need to fix before moving on.

Adjusting the responsive navbar breakpoint

Our navbar, with the logo image, larger nav items, and icons, has grown in width. And a problem for our responsive design has arisen. Try resizing your browser window from wide to narrow (approx 480px) and back again, and chances are you'll see the navbar bump down under the logo at some point in the mid-range.

What's happened? The navbar has grown too wide for the container when our viewport is between 768px to 991px. This falls between the Bootstrap variables `@screen-sm-min` and `@screen-md-min`.

The `@grid-float-breakpoint` sets the point at which the navbar collapses. You'll find this variable in `_variables.less`, under the `// Grid system` section.

```
// Point at which the navbar stops collapsing
@grid-float-breakpoint:     @screen-sm-min;
```

We need to adjust this breakpoint so that the navbar stays collapsed until the next breakpoint: `@screen-md-min`. Update the variable accordingly:

```
@grid-float-breakpoint:     @screen-md-min; // edited
```

Save, compile, and refresh. You'll see that the navbar does in fact stay collapsed until the next breakpoint.

Problem solved! It's time to move on to the carousel.

Styling the carousel

We're going to take Bootstrap's default carousel styles and apply some significant customization. Let's create a copy of Bootstrap's `carousel.less` file and make it our own.

1. Copy `bootstrap/carousel.less` and save it in the `less` directory as `_carousel.less`.

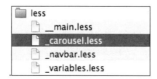

2. Update the relevant import line in `__main.less` to import our custom file in place of Bootstrap's:

```
@import "_carousel.less";
```

3. Customize the opening comment in `_feature-carousel.less`:

```
//
// Customized Carousel
// --------------------------------------------------
```

Now to begin customizing!

Setting Font Awesome icons for the controls

If you unhooked Glyphicons as I did in the preceding section, you'll find that the next and previous carousel controls have disappeared. This is because they relied on Glyphicons. We can fix this using Font Awesome icons instead.

1. First, update the icons markup in `index.html`. Look for the links with the classes `left` or `right` and `carousel-control`:

```
<a class="left carousel-control" ...
```

2. Update the `span` tags with a generic icon class, plus the Font Awesome icon classes as follows:

```
<span class="icon fa fa-chevron-left"></span>
...
<span class="icon fa fa-chevron-right"></span>
```

3. Next, we need to add new class selectors in `_carousel.less`. You'll find it under the selector `.carousel-control`, beneath the comment for `// Toggles`. I'll paste the block of code with the necessary updates and comments:

```
// Toggles
  .icon-prev,
  .icon-next,
  .glyphicon-chevron-left,
  .glyphicon-chevron-right,
  .icon {   // added
    position: absolute;
    top: 50%;
    z-index: 5;
    display: inline-block;
  }
```

```
.icon-prev,
.glyphicon-chevron-left,
&.left .icon { // added
  left: 20%; // edited was 50%
}
.icon-next,
.glyphicon-chevron-right,
&.right .icon { // added
  right: 20%; // edited was 50%
}
```

Three notes about these edits:

- By using a basic `icon` class both in the markup and here, we may use any icon of our choice and our styles will still work
- The `&.left` and `&.right` constructions reach back in the nesting hierarchy and compile to `.carousel-control.left` and `.carousel-control.right`
- By altering the value for the `left:` and `right:` positions, I've nudged the icons closer to the edges of the carousel

Save, compile, and refresh. Our new Font Awesome icons should take their appropriate places.

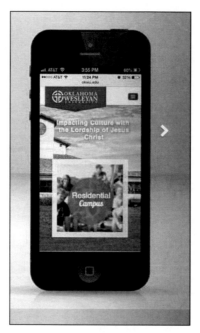

Now, we can move on to aesthetic enhancements.

Adding top and bottom padding

Let's add some top and bottom padding to the `.carousel` element itself and add our `@gray-lighter` color for a background color. To help keep track of my work, I'm going to tack on a small comment at the end of each added or edited line. (Again, these will never make it to CSS!)

```
.carousel {
  position: relative;
  padding-top: 4px; // added
  padding-bottom: 28px; // added
  background-color: @gray-lighter; // added
}
```

After saving and compiling, you'll see the light gray background appears in our newly created space above and below the carousel images. This provides a bit of framing to set them off from the other elements above and below. In a bit, we'll take advantage of the extra bottom padding to position our carousel indicators in a way that allows them to stand out much more clearly.

First, let's ensure that our images will stretch to fill their space in all circumstances.

Forcing images to their full width

We need to force our images to stretch the full width of the carousel, even in wide screens. Our images are 1600px wide to fill most screens. But beyond this width, they will leave a gap at the right edge.

Forcing the images to their full width on windows wider than 1600px may pixelate them slightly; but for images that are large enough, distortions won't be huge.

 When time allows, we can add a responsive image solution to load smaller images on smaller screens; and if we desire, we can add larger images for these wider sizes. I'll get you rolling with a responsive image solution in *Appendix B, Implementing Responsive Images*.

For now, we need to add only two lines to our file. Just below the rules for the `.carousel` selector are the nested set of rules we need for this. Under the `.carousel-inner` selector are rules for carousel images, including a mixin which ensures they behave responsively and adjust to smaller screens. We can also force them to stretch wider for wider screens by setting `min-width:`.

```
.carousel-inner {
  ...
  > .item {
    ...
    > img,
    > a > img {
      .img-responsive();
      line-height: 1;
      min-width: 100%; // added
    }
  }
  ...
}
```

After implementing this adjustment, we can stretch our browser window as wide as we like, and the image will stretch along with it.

Next, we need to limit the maximum height of our carousel.

Constraining the carousel height

As you may have noticed, the carousel grows entirely too tall in the medium and large screen view. Our mock-ups call for a constrained height of approximately 440px. We can accomplish this easily by setting a constraint on the parent of our images, the `.carousel-inner > .item`, as follows:

```
.carousel-inner {
  ...
  > .item {
    ...
    max-height: 640px; // added
```

Because the `.carousel-inner` element has a rule of `overflow: hidden`, which constrains the height of the `.item` element, it serves as a convenient way to hide the lower portions of the image when it grows beyond the desired height.

Having done this, we can use nested media queries (another nice feature of LESS), along with Bootstrap's medium and large breakpoint variables to adjust the vertical positioning of our images at the widest widths, to keep our designs in the focal area. I'll do it by using the following code:

```
> img,
> a > img {
  ...
  @media (min-width: @screen-md-min) {
    margin-top: -40px;
  }
  @media (min-width: @screen-lg-min) {
    margin-top: -60px;
  }
}
```

Save, compile, and refresh. You should see that our carousel is taking shape nicely and works well from narrow to wide viewport widths.

At a narrow width, it appears like the following:

And in a wide viewport, it looks like the following:

Now, to style the carousel indicators.

Repositioning the carousel indicators

The carousel indicators serve to inform the user how many slides are in our carousel, and highlight the current spot in the rotation. At present, these indicators are barely visible—languishing near the bottom center edge of our portfolio images.

Let's move these indicators into their own space, just below the image:

1. In `_carousel.less`, search for the selector `.carousel-indicator`. We want the first of its two occurrences, approximately 2/3 of the way down the file. This section opens with a comment.

   ```
   // Optional indicator pips
   ```

   Notice how the element is vertically positioned.

   ```
   .carousel-indicators {
     position: absolute;
     bottom: 10px;
   ```

2. We want to move these down even closer to the bottom edge, into our light gray area created by the padding we added above. So, let's adjust the bottom positioning. In addition, we need to remove the default bottom margin by zeroing it out.

```
.carousel-indicators {
  position: absolute;
  bottom: 0; // edited
  margin-bottom: 0; // added
```

3. Save, compile, and test. You may notice that on small screen sizes, this positions our indicators where we want them. On larger screen sizes, however, they return to their previous position. As it turns out, this is the result of a rule under media query where we were just working — down near very bottom of the file.

4. Find these lines near the bottom of the file, within the media query for `@screen-tablet` and up.

```
// Move up the indicators
  .carousel-indicators {
    bottom: 20px;
  }
```

Since we no longer need this adjustment, let's simply comment out these lines, thereby removing them from the CSS altogether.

```
// .carousel-indicators {
//   bottom: 20px;
// }
```

This brings our desired result. The indicators now stay positioned in the desired space across all screen dimensions.

Now, let's update their appearance to make them larger and easier to see.

Styling the indicators

We'll make our carousel indicators more visible by using our gray variables. We'll also increase their size a bit. We can get a start in our `_variables.less` file.

1. In `_variables.less`, just after the `@carousel-control` variables, you'll find two variables beginning with `@carousel-indicator`:

    ```
    @carousel-indicator-active-bg:          #fff;
    @carousel-indicator-border-color:       #fff;
    ```

    These are used to provide a white border around the default indicators, and then fill the active indicator with the background color.

2. Let's add a default background color variable here, so that we may fill the default indicators with our `@gray-light` value.

    ```
    @carousel-indicator-bg:          @gray-light;
    ```

3. Then, we'll update the active background color.

    ```
    @carousel-indicator-active-bg:    @gray-lightest;
    ```

4. Finally, we'll make the border-color transparent.

    ```
    @carousel-indicator-border-color: transparent;
    ```

5. Save, compile, and refresh.

At present, this has the effect of making all but the active item invisible.

Now, for some work in `_carousel.less`.

1. In the file `_carousel.less`, move to the first set of rules for `.carousel-indicator` where we were previously working.

    ```
    .carousel-indicators {
      position: absolute;
      ...
    ```

2. Look for the `li` selector nested under it. Here, let's edit several values. Specifically, we'll perform the following actions:

    ○   Increase the width and height to 16px

    ○   Remove the margin

- ◦ Add `background-color` using our newly created variable @ `carousel-indicator-bg`
- ◦ Remove the border line altogether (the transparent value we set for the border variable is now merely a failsafe)
- ◦ I've commented these changes in the following code snippet

```
li {
    display: inline-block;
    width:   18px; // edited
    height: 18px; // edited
    // margin: 1px; // edited
    text-indent: -999px;
    background-color: @carousel-indicator-bg; // added
    // border: 1px solid @carousel-indicator-border-color;
    border-radius: 10px;
    ...
```

3. Notice the following hack for IE 8-9 to supply the indicators with a `background-color` for these browsers. Because we have just provided a background color for all of our indicators, this hack is no longer needed. Comment out these lines under the comment. Otherwise, these will interfere with our background color declaration in the preceding snippet.

```
    // background-color: #000 \9; // IE8
    // background-color: rgba(0,0,0,0); // IE9
```

4. Next, we need to remove the margin, width, and height values under the `.active` selector as we no longer want our active indicator to grow larger (nor do we want it to shrink back to 12px).

```
.active {
    // margin:  0; // edited
    // width:   12px; // edited
    // height: 12px; // edited
    background-color: @carousel-indicator-active-bg;
}
```

5. Finally, let's add a hover effect by adding a `:hover` selector along with the `.active` selector.

```
li:hover, // added
.active { ...
```

6.   Save, compile, and refresh. And check out the result!

Carousel adjustments accomplished! We've learned a lot in the process—a lot about Bootstrap and perhaps a little about LESS as well.

Let's move on to the next section. What's remaining is considerably simpler.

Tweaking the columns and their content

Let's fine-tune the blocks of content under the three headings **Welcome!**, **Recent Updates**, and **Our Team**.

First, let's add the arrow-circle icon to the button in each of these three blocks. Recall that we're using Font Awesome for our icon selection.

1.   Visit the Font Awesome documentation at `http://fortawesome.github.io/Font-Awesome/icons/`.

2.   You'll find the icon that we're after.

3. In `index.html`, add a span tag with the appropriate classes inside each link. Here is the first one, which I've spaced out by adding an extra carriage return between elements.

```
<p>
  <a class="btn btn-primary pull-right" href="#">
    See our portfolio <span class="icon fa fa-arrow-circle-
      right"></span>
  </a>
</p>
```

4. Repeat for each link.

You should now have the desired icon in each of the three buttons.

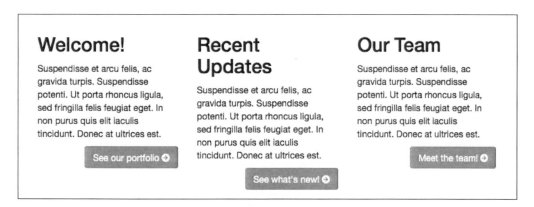

While we're at it, let's add a bit of vertical padding between the carousel and this section of text. Right now, it's pretty tight.

The question that comes up at this point is where best to compose the styles that we'll need for this. Adding extra padding around page content sections will likely be a pretty normal practice for us now and in the future. Let's create a LESS file to hold these and other tweaks to the ordinary contents of pages. (As it happens, we'll need this file for an additional and more important responsive adjustment, so it seems well justified.)

1. Create a file named `_page-contents.less`.

2. Save it in your `less` folder alongside your other custom less files.

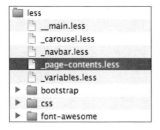

3. Comment the file.

    ```
    //
    // Page Contents
    // ------------------------
    ```

4. Then, let's create a sensible class for this purpose and add our desired padding—including some padding for the bottom.

    ```
    .page-contents {
      padding-top: 20px;
      padding-bottom: 40px;
    }
    ```

5. Save the file.

6. Add `_page-contents.less` to the imports in `__main.less`. I'll add mine in a new section near the bottom of the file, just before the **Utility** classes, and I'll include a helpful comment for orientation purposes.

    ```
    // Other custom files
    @import "_page-contents.less";
    ```

7. Save and compile.

8. Now, let's add the necessary class to our markup. Open `index.html` and add the class `page-contents` to the div with the class `container`, which follows just after the closing `div` of our `homepage-feature` carousel.

```
</div><!-- /#homepage-feature.carousel -->
<div class="page-contents container">
<div class="row">
```

9. Save and refresh your browser. You should see the padding added.

Next, we need to tidy up the narrow-screen view of these blocks. Notice that when viewed in single-column layout, the headings do not clear the floated buttons.

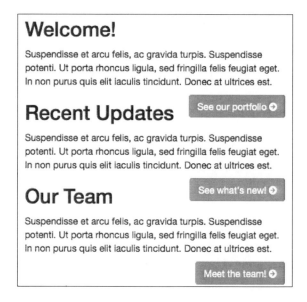

Fixing this is just a little tricky. We might want to add a clearfix to the div containing each of these three blocks. However, that won't work because we need these blocks to float side by side once the viewport width is 768px or up.

This calls for a media query. Recalling that our three-column view begins at the `@screen-sm` breakpoint, or 768px, let's set a rule to clear floats when the window is one pixel below this breakpoint—which is the purpose of the special breakpoint `@screen-xs-max`. You'll find these special `-max` breakpoints just below the other `@screen` variables in `_variables.less`.

```
// So media queries don't overlap when required, provide a maximum
@screen-xs-max:          (@screen-sm - 1);
@screen-sm-max:          (@screen-md - 1);
@screen-md-max:          (@screen-lg - 1);
```

The `@screen-xs-max` breakpoint is what we need in this case, as it provides a value one pixel narrower than the `@screen-sm` breakpoint.

 Using the `@screen-sm-min` variable would leave a 1px zone in which the columns would stay approximately a third of width, but would be too wide for the columns to float side by side. This causes the columns to stack on top of each other. Not the result we want. In my testing, this 1px overlap broke the layout on the iPad. So, the `@screen-xs-max` variable is important!

While we're at it, let's also add some bottom padding to our columns so that they have a bit of extra vertical breathing room when stacked.

Inside our media query, we'll add a CSS2 attribute selector to select all elements with a class that contains `col-`, so that the same rules will apply to a column of any size:

```
.page-contents {
...
@media (max-width: @screen-xs-max) {
  [class*="col-"] {
    clear: both;
    padding-bottom: 40px;
  }
}
}
```

Save, compile, and refresh. The result is much improved!

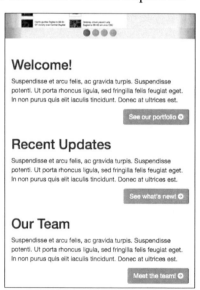

Much better!

Now, let's move on to the footer!

Styling the footer

The biggest feature of the footer is our social icons. Font Awesome to the rescue!

Consulting the Font Awesome documentation, we find a slew of available icons under the category of **Brand Icons**. Here is the direct link:

```
http://fortawesome.github.io/Font-Awesome/icons/#brand
```

Now, we only need to replace the text for each social link in our footer with span elements, using the appropriate classes.

```html
<ul class="social">
  <li><a href="#" title="Twitter Profile"><span class="icon fa
    fa-twitter"></span></a></li>
  <li><a href="#" title="Facebook Page"><span class="icon fa
    fa-facebook"></span></a></li>
  <li><a href="#" title="LinkedIn Profile"><span class="icon fa
    fa-linkedin"></span></a></li>
  <li><a href="#" title="Google+ Profile"><span class="icon fa fa-
    google-plus"></span></a></li>
  <li><a href="#" title="GitHub Profile"><span class="icon fa fa-
    github-alt"></span></a></li>
</ul>
```

This updated markup puts our icons in place:

Now, perform the following steps to lay them out horizontally and align them to the center.

1. Create a new file _footer.less to manage these styles.

2. Save the file to the `less` directory.

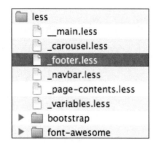

3. Add an import variable for this file in `__main.less`.

```less
// Other custom files
@import "_page-contents.less";
@import "_footer.less";
```

Now, we'll write the styles we need. Let me simply lay them out, and then list what they do.

The lines that we'll need are given as follows:

```less
ul.social {
  margin: 0;
  padding: 0;
  width: 100%;
  text-align: center;
  > li {
    display: inline-block;
    > a {
      display: inline-block;
      font-size: 18px;
      line-height: 30px;
      .square(30px); // see bootstrap/mixins.less
      border-radius: 36px;
      background-color: @gray-light;
      color: #fff;
      margin: 0 3px 3px 0;
        &:hover {
        text-decoration: none;
        background-color: @link-hover-color;
        }
      }
    }
  }
}
```

Here's what's happening:

- The normal margin and padding is stripped away from the `ul`
- It is stretched to a 100 percent width
- Its content is center aligned
- The list items are displayed inline block, thereby centering them
- The links are displayed inline block, so that they fill up their available space
- The font size and line height are increased
- The width and height are set to 30px square, using a Bootstrap provided mixin
- To see this mixin, open `bootstrap/mixins.less`, search for `.square`, and you'll find the following relevant lines:

  ```
  // Sizing shortcuts
  .size(@width; @height) {
    width: @width;
    height: @height;
  }
  .square(@size) {
    .size(@size; @size);
  }
  ```

- The `border-radius` property is set large enough to make the icons and their backgrounds appear circular
- The background color, color, and margin properties are set
- The underline is removed from the hover state, and the background color is altered to a lighter gray

With these steps accomplished, let's polish off the footer by adding a healthy bit of top and bottom padding, and then center aligning the content in order to move our logo to the center above the social icons.

```
footer[role="contentinfo"] {
  padding-top: 24px`;
  padding-bottom: 36px;
  text-align: center;
}
```

The result is as follows:

Not bad — if I don't say so myself!

Recommended next steps

Let me strongly recommend at least one additional next step you'll need to take before taking a project like this to production. It's imperative that you take time to optimize your images, CSS, and JavaScript. These steps are not difficult.

- Compressing images takes just a bit of time, and it addresses the single largest cause for large page footprints. I've already used the save to web process option of Photoshop, but chances are you can squeeze a few more bytes out.

- In addition, we badly need to remove unneeded Bootstrap LESS files from the import sequence in __main.less, and then compress the resulting main.css file.

- Finally, we need to slim down our plugins.js file by replacing Bootstrap's all-inclusive bootstrap.min.js file with compressed versions of only the three plugins that we're actually using: carousel.js, collapse.js, and transitions.js. We then compress the final plugins.js file.

Combined, these steps can cut the footprint of this website by roughly half. In an age where speed matters — both for user retention and for SEO ranking — that's a big deal. To help you in this task, I've included steps for optimizing this project in *Appendix A, Optimizing Site Assets*.

In addition, there are two other very sensible steps you may want to take.

First, we can implement a responsive images technique to further optimize our carousel images. Those images, as you'll recall, are too large (unnecessarily large) to send to small-screen devices. Conversely, if we want the images to look crisp on large retina screens, we might opt to provide higher-resolution versions for those displays. In *Appendix B*, *Implementing Responsive Images*, I'll walk you through the implementation of Scott Jehl's excellent **Picturefill** solution.

Second, we know that users of touch-enabled devices appreciate the ability to swipe their way forward and back through a carousel. In *Appendix C*, *Adding Swipe to the Carousel*, I'll show you how to use the excellent `Hammer.js` plugin to enable swipe interaction with our carousel in just a few steps.

But, for the present moment, let's stop and celebrate.

Summary

Let's take stock of what we've accomplished in this chapter.

- We've begun with a rock-solid markup structure provided by the HTML5 Boilerplate
- We've leveraged Bootstrap's responsive navbar, carousel, and grid system
- We've customized several of Bootstrap's LESS files
- We've created our own LESS files and folded them seamlessly into the project
- We've doubled our available icons by folding Font Awesome into our workflow
- We've improved future maintenance of the site by implementing a thoughtful file organization scheme and leaving a trail of helpful comments—all without creating code bloat

With this experience under your belt, you're equipped to bend Bootstrap to your will—using its power to speed website development, and then customizing the design to your heart's content. In future chapters, we'll expand your experience further. First, however, let's take this design and turn it into a WordPress theme.

3
Bootstrappin' a WordPress Theme

Now let's turn our design from *Chapter 2, Bootstrappin' Your Portfolio*, into a WordPress theme. There are many Bootstrap-based themes that we could choose. We've taken care to integrate Bootstrap's powerful LESS styles and JavaScript plugins with the best practices found in the HTML5 Boilerplate. It will be to our advantage to use a theme that does the same.

The Roots theme has established itself as a starter theme that leverages the power of Bootstrap while hewing to the implementation of best practices at every turn, including the HTML5 Boilerplate among other excellent touches. We'll use this theme for this exercise.

In this chapter, we will perform the following:

- Integrate our customized LESS and JavaScript files with the Roots theme
- Customize the theme template files to deliver the markup we need for our home page carousel and column content
- Utilize the powerful and advanced custom fields plugin to provide custom fields for our carousel items and home page columns
- Create a home page template file that publishes our custom fields into our desired home page layout

Downloading and renaming the Roots theme

Let's get started by downloading the Roots theme:

1. Navigate to the Roots theme home page at `http://roots.io/`.

   You might take some time to familiarize yourself with the resources here. (It's a great and growing development community.)

2. Proceed on to the GitHub project by clicking on the GitHub link. The direct URL is `https://github.com/roots/roots`.

3. Download the ZIP file.

4. Extract it.

5. Rename the extracted folder to your desired theme name as shown in the following screenshot:

6. Navigate inside the main theme folder to the `style.css` file as shown in the following screenshot, and open it in your editor:

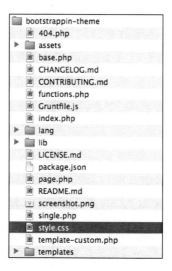

7. Once you've opened the file, you'll notice that it contains no actual styles. Site styles are provided by a stylesheet `css` folder located inside the `assets` folder, which is compiled by Bootstrap. We'll follow this approach as well. The `style.css` file then serves primarily to name our theme, give appropriate credits, declare the license, and so on. So, let's do that.

8. Change the comments to reflect your new theme information. Here's what I've done with some hints for you:

```
/*
Theme Name:        Bootstrappin' Theme
Theme URI:         [your site URI]
Description:       A custom theme based on <a href="http://www.
roots.io">the Roots Theme</a>
Version:           1.0
Author:            [Your Name Here]
Author URI:        [Your URL]

License:           [Supply your chosen license]
License URI:       [Supply license URI]
*/
```

9. Save the file.

10. Now let's add a custom screenshot so that we can recognize the theme in the WordPress Dashboard.

11. Grab a screenshot from our results in *Chapter 2, Bootstrappin' Your Portfolio*. (I've provided one in the `03_Code_BEGIN` exercise files folder.)

12. Replace the default Roots screenshot with our new custom screenshot.

We now have our own copy of the Roots theme set up.

Let's install it!

Installing the theme

Be prepared. The changes that we made earlier have temporarily severed connections to Bootstrap styles, JavaScript, and so on. We're going to update these connections in the following steps. We're simply going to make the process more enjoyable by having the theme installed and running so that we can test our progress along the way!

1. Upload your new theme to your WordPress site's `themes` folder. (If you're working locally, simply make a copy of it or move it there.)

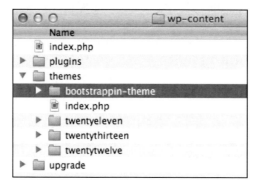

2. Then, from your WordPress Dashboard, navigate to **Appearance | Themes** and activate the theme. If you've renamed it and provided the new screenshot (or used the provided theme-starter files), you'll see something like the following screenshot:

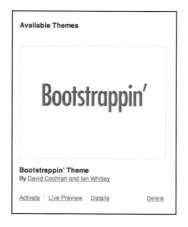

Available Themes

Bootstrappin'

Bootstrappin' Theme
By David Cochran and Ian Whitley

Activate | Live Preview | Details   Delete

3. You'll be taken to the activation page, which presents you with the following options. Here's how to consider answering them:

    ○   **Create static front page?**

        Yes

We'll use this for our home page.

    ○   **Change permalink structure?**

        Yes

This is one of the first settings we typically change so that URLs in our site use post and page names.

> In my own recent local MAMP installation process, I found that Roots theme paths did not work until I updated the permalink structure.

    ○   **Change uploads folder?**

        No

You can choose whether to change the folder where your uploads go or leave it as it is by default.

    ○   **Create navigation menu?**

        Yes

This sets up our top navigation

    ○   **Add pages to menu?**

        Yes

That'd be great. Thank you!

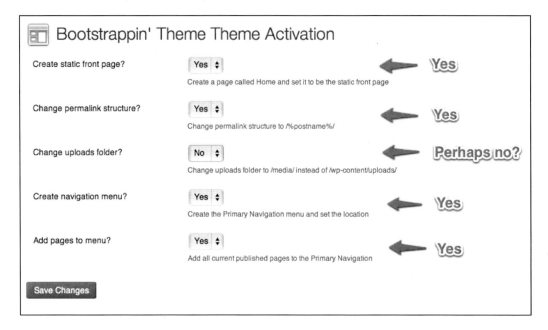

 If you notice the alert to make sure your `.htaccess` file is writable, this can be resolved by creating an `.htaccess` file in the `root` folder of your WordPress site (not the `themes` folder but the main folder containing `wp-content`, `wp-admin`, and so on) and ensuring that permissions are set to `664`.

4. Save changes.

5. You'll be taken back to the **Appearance | Themes** management page.

6. Click on the **Customize** link.

7. You'll be taken to a page where you can set up several basic options quickly as follows:

  ° **Site Title & Tagline**: Update your tagline

  ° **Navigation**: Update if needed

  ° **Static Front Page**: Update if needed

8. In the right-hand side pane, you should see the default Bootstrap navbar, a heading, and a long paragraph of filler text.

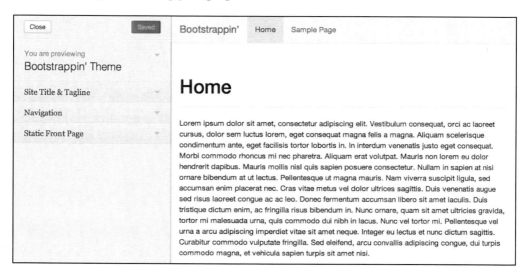

Congratulations! You've got the Roots theme installed.

If you do not see the default Bootstrap styles applied to the navbar or text, this is a sign that the Roots theme has gotten its file paths confused. Often, this can be cleared up by resetting your permalinks settings by navigating to **Settings | Permalinks**.

Let's set up our navbar items.

Configuring the navbar

In this section, we'll set up the navbar items for our site pages, and we'll also go ahead and add the markup for our icons:

1. In your WordPress Dashboard, navigate to **Appearance | Menus**.

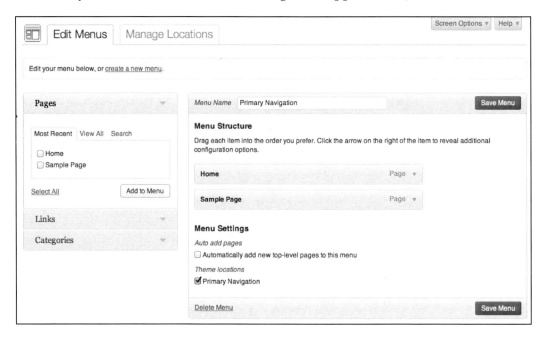

2. Remove the **Sample Page** menu item from the menu.

3. Edit the **Home** menu item by adding the markup for our Font Awesome icon to the **label** area using the same markup from our *Chapter 2, Bootstrappin' Your Portfolio*, `index.html` file shown as follows:

    ```
    <span class="icon fa fa-home"></span> Home
    ```

4. Now create the remainder of your pages—for now, you could do so by creating simple custom links—using the appropriate markup as the label for each page.

5. The **Link Text** fields for each menu item are as follows:

```
<span class="icon fa fa-desktop"></span> Portfolio
<span class="icon fa fa-group"></span> Team
<span class="icon fa fa-envelope"></span> Contact
```

6. After adding each one to its menu, save the menu.

Recall that our Font Awesome icons are not yet available. Bootstrap does not provide them by default, and neither does the Roots theme. So, our icons will not appear until we supply our new site assets in a later step ahead.

7. Now go ahead and refresh the home page and you will see the link text appear.

It's now time to put our home page content in place.

Bringing in our home page content

As we contemplate how to bring our home page content into WordPress, two possible methods leap to mind:

- **WYSIWYG dump**: Copying and pasting the entire markup structure for our carousel and columns into the visual editor and then uploading our images and placing them within the context of that markup structure.

- **Custom fields**: Using WordPress custom fields to enter our key elements — the carousel images and the column content — and then customizing a template file to provide our desired markup structure.

The first approach is not a good long-term solution as the visual or WYSIWYG editor is not adept at handling complex markup structure. Nevertheless, this approach *is* the quickest, and in this case, it will help us with our first steps. So, let's begin quick and dirty, if you will, and we'll clean things up with the custom fields method nearer the end.

In the exercise files for this chapter, you will find the files from our *Chapter 2, Bootstrappin' Your Portfolio*, Portfolio results. We'll use the `index.html` file to get the markup we need for our carousel and columns:

1. In the `index.html` file from *Chapter 2, Bootstrappin' Your Portfolio*, copy the entire block of code inside the opening and closing `main` tags, *but not including* the `main` tags themselves:
   - We'll begin with the beginning of the carousel:
     ```
     <div id="homepage-feature" class="carousel slide">
     ```
   - And we'll select everything, including the three columns and the `div` tags of class `row` and `container` that surround them, which takes us down through the last closing `div` tag just before the closing `</main>` tag.

2. Copy the block we just selected in the last step, but *do not* paste it into WordPress yet. We need to clean it up a bit. Recall that WordPress wants to add paragraph tags around any content that seems to need it. So, we need to remove elements that might trigger this behavior.

3. Paste this block of code into a new window of your code editor.

4. Remove indentation as indentation will make it very difficult for us to manage the code once we paste it into the WordPress visual editor. Select the entire block of code and shift everything as far left as it can go so that each line starts at the far left with no indentation.

5. Then, remove any comments that take a line of their own. I had the following two comments:
   ```
   <!-- Wrapper for slides -->
   <!-- Controls -->
   ```

6. Also, remove any blank line. I had a blank line above each of the preceding comments.

7. Copy your cleaned-up block of code.

8. In your WordPress Dashboard, go to **Edit Pages** and edit the page named **Home**.

9. Before pasting, shift from the visual editor to the text editor by clicking on the **Text** tab in the upper-right corner of the editor window as shown in the following screenshot:

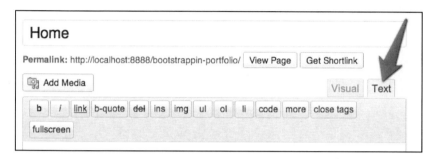

10. Now paste the markup into the editor.

That's a start. Now we need to upload our images.

Adding images

Let's upload our images into WordPress and insert them into the appropriate place in our markup:

1. You'll find the portfolio images plus the logo image in the img folder from the files in *Chapter 2, Bootstrappin' Your Portfolio,* Portfolio project as shown in the following screenshot:

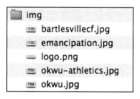

2. In your WordPress page editor for the **Home** page, click on the **Add Media** button to upload your images into WordPress.

3. Select and upload the four portfolio images as shown in the following screenshot:

4. Set appropriate settings for each image as follows:

    ○ Provide a suitable **Alt Text** attribute

    ○ Set **Alignment** to **None**

    ○ For now, we can remove the hyperlink entirely (although, of course, your portfolio items will likely link to a page about that project)

    ○ Select the full-size version of the image

5. Insert the full-size (1600 pixel) version of each image in its appropriate place in the markup, replacing the former image tag with the new one.

    Consider the following line of code:

    ```
    <img src="img/okwu.jpg" alt="OKWU.edu Homepage">
    ```

    It will now become something like the following code snippet (with the `src` attribute varying according to the location of your WordPress installation):

    ```
    <img src="http://localhost:8888/bootstrappin-portfolio/wp-content/
    uploads/2013/10/okwu.jpg" alt="OKWU.edu Homepage" width="1600"
    height="800" class="alignnone size-full wp-image-29" />
    ```

    Repeat this process for each of the four images.

6. Now, with your markup and images in place, update the page!

7. Go to your site **Home** page and refresh it. If all went well, you should see the carousel and columns appear as shown in the following screenshot:

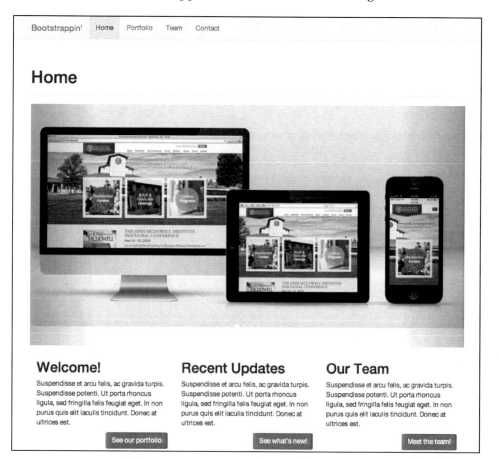

We've got the majority of our home page content in place. You'll notice default Bootstrap styles in the colors, carousel dimensions, and other details. We'll soon swap our updated design assets into place to fix this. First, let's address a couple of template matters.

We have a page title that we don't need—a feature of the standard Roots page template. And our carousel is being constrained to the same width as the columns after it. If we inspect the page elements, we'll see that the page template has wrapped our entire page content within an element that uses the Bootstrap class `container` to constrain its width.

```
▼<div class="wrap container" role="document">
  ▼<div class="content row">
    ▼<div class="main col-sm-12" role="main">
```

We need to adjust our templates to remove the page title and set the carousel free from its container.

Customizing a page template

On an average page, we may want to display the page title. The home page is a special page of course. Let's prepare a custom template for it.

In the following steps, we'll set up a custom page template that will remove the page heading and bring in a custom template for our page contents. We'll equip the custom content template with the markup structure we need for the carousel and columns:

1. In the main `themes` folder, find the `template-custom.php` file. This is a sample page template that's easy for us to adapt.

2. Make a copy of it and rename it `page-home.php` as shown in the following screenshot:

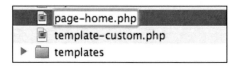

3. Open the new `page-home.php` file in your editor and edit the opening comment, changing the template name to `Homepage Template`:

```
/*
Template Name: Homepage Template
*/
```

4. Save the file.

5. Now, back in your WordPress Dashboard, edit the page named **Home**. Change its page template to the newly created `Homepage Template`.

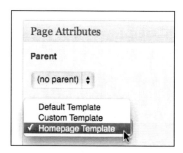

6. Update the page.

7. There is no need to view the page in your browser yet as nothing will be different. Let's first make a change to the template.

8. In your code editor, with `page-home.php` open, find the following line of code:

```
<?php get_template_part('templates/page', 'header'); ?>
```

9. This is the first of two lines of PHP. This first line pulls in the page title. (The template for this is found in the `page-header.php` file inside the `templates` folder.) Thus, we can remove the page title by simply removing the first line or commenting it out. Here I've used a single-line comment to comment out the call for the page header as follows:

```
<?php // get_template_part('templates/page', 'header'); ?>
<?php get_template_part('templates/content', 'page'); ?>
```

10. Save the file. View and refresh the **Home** page in your browser. You should see the page title disappear as shown in the following screenshot:

That's a start! Now to free our carousel from its bounding container element.

Understanding the Roots base template

One of the impressive things about the Roots theme is that it has pulled the fundamental layout elements out of individual template files and placed them into a file named base.php. We'll look at this in just a moment.

First, let's notice that the base.php file receives instructions on fundamental layout matters from the config.php file inside the lib folder. Take a moment to open this latter file and scan through it. I will not touch upon everything here. You can read more about the details in the following two pages in the Roots documentation:

- The *Roots 101* page at http://roots.io/roots-101

- The *An Introduction to the Roots Theme Wrapper* page at http://roots.io/an-introduction-to-the-roots-theme-wrapper/

For present purposes, note that we have the ability to specify what class should be put on the main column and the sidebar as well as to determine the pages that should *not* have a standard sidebar.

If you search for the phrase main class, you'll find lines that set the main and sidebar classes. If the page has a sidebar, the main element will receive the col-sm-8 class, limiting its width to two-thirds the width of the container, while the sidebar receives the col-sm-4 class. If there is no sidebar, the main columns will receive the col-sm-12 class and will be made full width.

```
/**
 * .main classes
 */
function roots_main_class() {
  if (roots_display_sidebar()) {
    // Classes on pages with the sidebar
    $class = 'col-sm-8';
  } else {
    // Classes on full width pages
    $class = 'col-sm-12';
  }
  return $class;
}
/**
 * .sidebar classes
 */
function roots_sidebar_class() {
  return 'col-sm-4';
}
```

The classes mentioned in the previous code snippet assume that we want the transition from a single-column to a multi-column layout to occur at the `@screen-sm` breakpoint. We can easily change that here. We can also easily change the widths of our main column and sidebar by updating these classes, which is to say that we can update the layout for all pages and posts from this single location, making the results effective throughout our site without having to combine multiple template files. While at first this arrangement may seem confusing, it is a huge efficiency gain.

Next, notice how the `config.php` file determines which pages receive a sidebar or actually, which pages should not, as shown in the following code snippet:

```php
/**
 * Define which pages shouldn't have the sidebar
 * ...
 */
function roots_display_sidebar() {
  $sidebar_config = new Roots_Sidebar(

    array(
      'is_404',
      'is_front_page'
    ),
    ...
    array(
      'template-custom.php'
    )
  );
  return apply_filters('roots_display_sidebar', $sidebar_config-
>display);
}
```

Thus, by default, the front page, 404 page, and any page that uses the custom page template will not receive a sidebar. We can easily add or remove pages and templates to this list, making it possible to customize the layout in entire sections of our site or individually as needed.

With this in mind, we're ready to look at `base.php`. Find this file in the main `themes` folder and open it in your editor.

Scan down through it and you will notice that this file does the following things:

- It pulls in the head of the page—see the `head.php` file in the `templates` folder.

    ```php
    <?php get_template_part('templates/head'); ?>
    ```

- It supplies the body tag and body classes.

```
<body <?php body_class(); ?>>
```

- It pulls in either the top navbar or a header with normal navigation—see the `header-top-navbar.php` and `header.php` templates.

```php
<?php
  do_action('get_header');
  // Use Bootstrap's navbar if enabled in config.php
  if (current_theme_supports('bootstrap-top-navbar')) {
    get_template_part('templates/header-top-navbar');
  } else {
    get_template_part('templates/header');
  }
?>
```

- If you jump down to the bottom, you'll see that it pulls in the footer—see the `footer.php` file in the `templates` folder.

```php
<?php get_template_part('templates/footer'); ?>
```

- And in the middle of all this, we see the block of code that defines the structure for the page content:

    ○ Begins with a container and a row:

```
<div class="wrap container" role="document">
  <div class="content row">
```

    ○ Defines `div class` as `main` with a `roots_main_class` method that sets the column width:

```
<div class="main <?php echo roots_main_class(); ?>"
role="main">
```

 The `roots_main_class` method is defined in the `config.php` file in the `lib` folder.

    ○ Uses the appropriate template for the content of the present page:

```php
<?php include roots_template_path(); ?>
```

    ○ Closes the `div` tag for `.main`:

```
</div><!-- /.main -->
```

○ Displays the sidebar, if called for, with its appropriate Bootstrap column class:

```
<?php if (roots_display_sidebar()) : ?>
  <aside class="sidebar <?php echo
    roots_sidebar_class(); ?>" role="complementary">
    <?php include roots_sidebar_path(); ?>
  </aside><!-- /.sidebar -->
<?php endif; ?>
```

 The config.php file establishes the pages that will have sidebars and the class that will be assigned to the sidebar.

○ And then closes up the row and container classes that have been applied respectively to the div tag of the content and wrap classes:

```
</div><!-- /.content -->
</div><!-- /.wrap -->
```

That's a lot to take in. Let's boil it down to this:

- The Roots base template lays out everything between the navbar and the footer within an element with the Bootstrap container class, thus constraining its width and keeping it from stretching full-width

- We need to set our carousel free to range the full width and then supply the container class when and where we want it

To fix this situation, we could simply remove the container class from the base template and adjust other elements accordingly. This would work except that our home page is the only one where we need the full-width carousel. So, we may inadvertently create more work for ourselves later by messing with the standard template file.

Instead, to accomplish our goal in a more targeted way, let's create a custom base template specifically for the home page. Roots makes it easy to do this.

Creating a custom base template

As a further testament to the power of the Roots theme, while the base.php file dictates fundamental layout for the entire site, we have the freedom to set up a custom base template to customize the fundamental layout structure when and where needed. We'll do that for our home page as shown in the following steps:

1. Duplicate the base.php file.

2. Name the new copy `base-page-home.php`. Because our page uses the `page-home.php` template file, Roots will check for a base template file by this name, and if it is found, Roots uses this file as the template for our home page.

 For more information on this base-template-choosing function, see the Roots documentation at `http://roots.io/an-introduction-to-the-roots-theme-wrapper/`.

3. Open the new `base-page-home.php` file in your editor.

4. Find the `div` tag of the `wrap` class and remove the `container` class from it so that it now reads as follows:

```
<div class="wrap" role="document">
```

5. We'll provide the `container` class where we need it, specifically for our columns below the carousel. The same goes for the `row` and `column` classes. So, we'll remove those from this template as well.

6. Just after this is the `div` tag of the `content` class; remove the `row` class so that this line now reads simply as follows:

```
<div class="content">
```

7. Finally, we need to remove the `php` tag from `div class` as `main` as we don't need the Bootstrap `column` class provided by `roots_main_class`. This line should now simply read as follows:

```
<div class="main" role="main">
```

8. Save your results.

9. Refresh the **Home** page in your browser.

    You should see the carousel expand to full width.

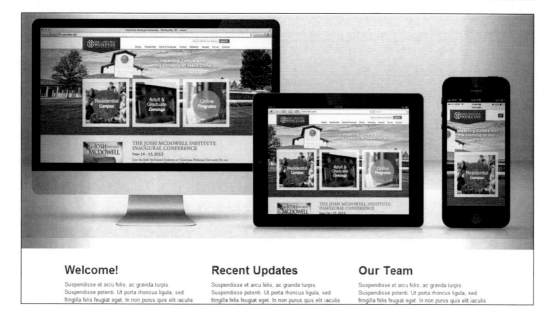

That's the magic!

Recall that we have provided the `container`, `row`, and `column` classes we need for the columns in what we've pasted into the WYSIWYG editor. Thus, these are constrained as they should be.

We are almost ready to bring in our custom styles. First, before finishing with our markup, let's clean things up and make them easier to maintain.

Using custom fields for a custom structure

As noted previously, the WYSIWYG dump is not the best long-term strategy for our home page content. We have some significant custom markup structure in here. The WordPress editor was built to manage text and images—not containers, rows, columns, and carousel items. So, let's use WordPress custom fields to manage this content.

The steps are easy and straightforward. We'll create a custom field for the content of each carousel item (that is, our four images) and then a custom field for each column of content below it as shown in the following steps:

1. In your WordPress editor for the **Home** page, copy the markup for each image as shown in the following screenshot:

Then, create a custom field for each, naming them item1, item2, item3, and item4. After repeating for each one, you should have a result that looks like the following screenshot:

2. Now for our columns content. Let's call these `column1`, `column2`, and `column3`, and include the heading, paragraphs, and button markup together in one custom field for each column's content.

Note that the contents for each column include more than what is shown in the field. Drag one to open it wider, and it includes the entire content as shown in the following screenshot:

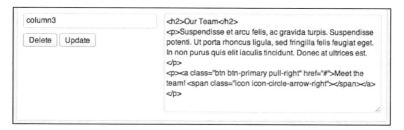

3. Update the page to save our work.

Now to pull the content from these fields and place them in our desired markup structure, which is to say, it's time for a bit more template work.

Creating a custom content template

We've established a custom base structure for our home page and set up a custom page template to remove the normal page title. Now it's time to create a custom template for our home page content.

Roots manages content loops in files named `content-page.php`, `content-single.php`, and `content.php` in the `templates` folder as shown in the following screenshot:

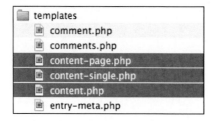

If you look at the contents of these files, you'll see the loops for standard posts and pages.

We want to make our own custom version of `content-page.php`:

1. Duplicate `content-page.php`.

2. Rename it `content-home.php`.

3. Open `content-home.php` in your editor and you'll see the following lines of code:

    ```php
    <?php while (have_posts()) : the_post(); ?>
      <?php the_content(); ?>
      <?php wp_link_pages(array('before' => '<nav
        class="pagination">', 'after' => '</nav>')); ?>
    <?php endwhile; ?>
    ```

4. Observe that this page content loop does two things:
    -   Pulls in the content from the WYSIWYG editor
    -   Creates links for paginated pages (if needed)

5. We want to update this loop to pull in our custom fields in place of the WYSIWYG editor. So, remove the following line:

    ```php
    <?php the_content(); ?>
    ```

6. We will not be paginating the home page, so remove the following line as well:

    ```php
    <?php wp_link_pages(array('before' => '<nav
      class="pagination">', 'after' => '</nav>')); ?>
    ```

    In their place, let's put a bit of alternative content so that we can test things.

7. Type something like `Hello this is a test!`.

8. Now we need to instruct our `page-home.php` template to use this new content loop.

9. Open `page-home.php` in your editor.

10. Edit the following line:

    ```php
    <?php get_template_part('templates/content', 'page'); ?>
    ```

    Replace `'page'` with `'home'` so that it now reads like the following line:

    ```php
    <?php get_template_part('templates/content', 'home'); ?>
    ```

    This instructs the template to pull our new content file, `content-home.php`, in the `templates` folder.

11. Save the changes.

12. Refresh the **Home** page.

    You should now see nothing but a line of text and the default footer.

Congratulations! Your new content template is connected. Now, to flesh it out, we will build a carousel from our new fields.

Building our carousel from custom fields

We want to pull the markup for our carousel items from their respective custom fields. If you've not worked with custom fields before, see the WordPress documentation at `http://codex.wordpress.org/Custom_Fields`.

We'll start by requesting the items themselves as follows:

1. With the `content-home.php` file in your editor, remove the test message. You should now have nothing except the following lines of code:

    ```php
    <?php while (have_posts()) : the_post(); ?>

    <?php endwhile; ?>
    ```

2. What we write next needs to be placed between these lines, and thus within the page loop.

3. To get our first carousel item, we need to ask for the content of the custom field called `item1`. The following line will do it:

```php
<?php $item="item1"; echo get_post_meta($post->ID, $item, true); ?>
```

This line first creates a PHP variable for `item1` and then uses that variable in the `get_post_meta()` template tag. The parameters `$post->ID`, `$item`, and `true` specify that we're working with the current post (or page) and asking for the field named `item1` to be returned as a string. (The `false` parameter would return it as an array.)

4. Save this file. Refresh your **Home** page and you should see the first image appear as shown in the following screenshot:

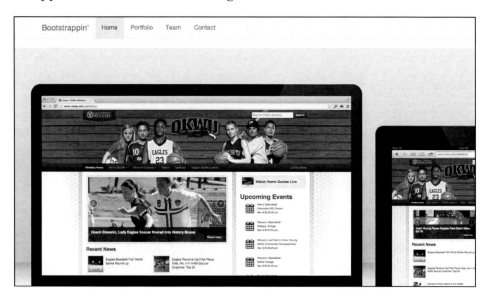

5. Now we need only to repeat the same line, updating each one to pull the next item. We need only to update the variable definition at the front of each line.

```php
<?php $item="item1"; echo get_post_meta($post->ID, $item,
   true); ?>
<?php $item="item2"; echo get_post_meta($post->ID, $item,
   true); ?>
<?php $item="item3"; echo get_post_meta($post->ID, $item,
   true); ?>
<?php $item="item4"; echo get_post_meta($post->ID, $item,
   true); ?>
```

If you save and refresh, you should see the images all appear, stretching down the page one after the other.

It's time now to wrap these items with our carousel markup. (Remember, you'll find this back in our original `index.html` file as well as in the WYSIWYG editor.)

6. We'll start with the fundamental parent `div` followed by the carousel indicators as shown in the following code snippet:

```
<?php while (have_posts()) : the_post(); ?>
  <div id="homepage-feature" class="carousel slide">
    <ol class="carousel-indicators">
      <li data-target="#homepage-feature" data-slide-to="0"
        class="active"></li>
      <li data-target="#homepage-feature" data-slide-
        to="1"></li>
      <li data-target="#homepage-feature" data-slide-
        to="2"></li>
      <li data-target="#homepage-feature" data-slide-
        to="3"></li>
    </ol>
```

7. Then, we'll begin the `carousel-inner` element and wrap each of our custom field tags in `div class` as `item`, the first one with the `active` class as shown in the following code snippet:

```
<div class="carousel-inner">
  <div class="item active">
    <?php $item="item1"; echo get_post_meta($post->ID,
      $item, true); ?>
  </div>
  <div class="item">
    <?php $item="item2"; echo get_post_meta($post->ID,
      $item, true); ?>
  </div>
  <div class="item">
    <?php $item="item3"; echo get_post_meta($post->ID,
      $item, true); ?>
  </div>
  <div class="item">
    <?php $item="item4"; echo get_post_meta($post->ID,
      $item, true); ?>
  </div>
</div><!-- /.carousel-inner -->
```

8. And we'll finish with the carousel controls.

```
<!-- Controls -->
  <a class="left carousel-control" href="#homepage-feature"
    data-slide="prev">
```

```
        <span class="icon-prev"></span>
        </a>
        <a class="right carousel-control" href="#homepage-
          feature" data-slide="next">
        <span class="icon-next"></span>
        </a>
      </div><!-- /#homepage-feature.carousel -->
```

9. With the carousel markup in place, save the file.

    Refresh your browser and you should see the functioning carousel again!

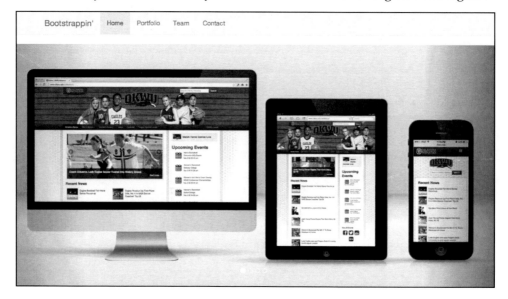

Now we just need to pull in our columns.

Adding our content columns from custom fields

To pull in the content for our three columns, we'll repeat a process very similar to the previous steps.

The following template tags will pull in the custom field for each column:

```
<?php $column="column1"; echo get_post_meta($post->ID, $column,
  true); ?>
<?php $column="column2"; echo get_post_meta($post->ID, $column,
  true); ?>
<?php $column="column3"; echo get_post_meta($post->ID, $column,
  true); ?>
```

Then, we need only to nest these within our markup structure—including the `container`, `row`, and `column` classes.

```
<div class="page-contents container">
    <div class="row">
        <div class="col-sm-4">
            <?php $column="column1"; echo get_post_meta($post->ID, $column,
true); ?>
        </div>
        <div class="col-sm-4">
            <?php $column="column2"; echo get_post_meta($post->ID, $column,
true); ?>
        </div>
        <div class="col-sm-4">
            <?php $column="column3"; echo get_post_meta($post->ID, $column,
true); ?>
        </div>
    </div><!-- /.row -->
</div><!-- /.container -->
```

Save your results, and you should see the three columns appear in their designated layout.

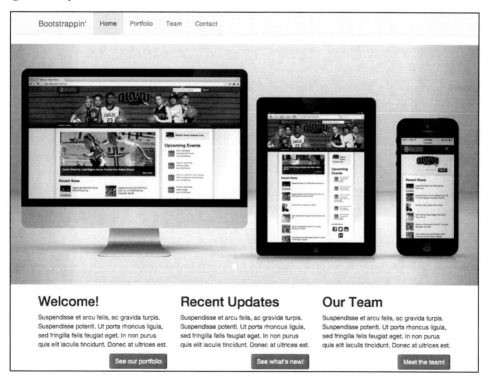

Next let's put our footer content in place.

Putting the footer content in place

Roots comes with a built-in footer widget area, which we can use to place the markup for our social icons:

1. In your WordPress Dashboard, go to **Appearance | Widgets**.

2. On the far right, beneath the **Primary** widget area, you'll see a widget area for the **Footer**.

3. Click on it to expand it.

4. Drag a **Text** widget into it.

5. Now, copy the markup for our social icons from the original `index.html` file as shown in the following code snippet:

```html
<ul class="social">
  <li><a href="#" title="Twitter Profile"><span class="icon fa fa-
twitter"></span></a></li>
  <li><a href="#" title="Facebook Page"><span class="icon fa fa-
facebook"></span></a></li>
  <li><a href="#" title="LinkedIn Profile"><span class="icon fa
fa-linkedin"></span></a></li>
  <li><a href="#" title="Google+ Profile"><span class="icon fa fa-
google-plus"></span></a></li>
  <li><a href="#" title="GitHub Profile"><span class="icon fa fa-
github-alt"></span></a></li>
</ul>
```

6. Paste this block of markup into the large text area.

7. Do not give it a title.

8. Do not check the **Automatically add paragraphs** checkbox.
9. Click on the **Save** button.
10. Refresh the **Home** page.

Recall that we've structured the icons in an unordered list. We've not yet added our custom styles nor our icon font, so you will likely see *only the bullets* of our unordered list appear.

Now, at last, it's time to put our custom site assets in place!

Before we swap out the Roots assets, let's pause to observe what's there. It will help the next steps make more sense.

Surveying the Roots assets folder

The Roots theme keeps its `css`, `less`, `js`, and `img` folders organized in its `assets` folder. Inside the `assets` folder, the structure is very similar to our structure from the *Chapter 2, Bootstrappin' Your Portfolio*, Portfolio site, as it is based, like ours, on the HTML5 Boilerplate.

We will soon replace Roots' assets with our own. But it's worth knowing how Roots works before we do so. Let's size up the contents of the Roots `assets` folder. The contents are shown in the following screenshot:

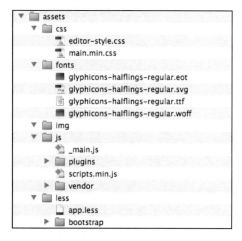

The Roots documentation (http://roots.io/roots-101/#theme-assets) explains how the files work together:

- In the less folder, the app.less file manages all style rules. It begins by importing all Bootstrap styles from the bootstrap.less file in the bootstrap folder and then provides commented sections with recommended selectors to write custom lines of LESS.

- The app.less file is intended to be compiled to the main.min.css file in the css folder.

- Also in the css folder is editor-style.css, which is used to supply custom styles to the WordPress visual editor.

- The js folder contains _main.js, which is intended to manage custom lines of JavaScript. (The file is equipped with a method to specify and limit the scope of lines of JavaScript to just the context(s) where needed.)

- The plugins folder inside the js folder holds all Bootstrap plugins, and is also intended to help manage any additional plugins.

- Like the HTML5 Boilerplate, the vendor folder contains essential standalone files and libraries, initially jQuery and Modernizr.

- Rather than combining plugins into a plugins.js file, the Roots strategy is to combine all plugins together with _main.js into a single file scripts.min.js.

In the Roots main folder is a Gruntfile, which can be used (dependent on the installation of Grunt on your system) to do the work of compiling LESS to CSS as well as combining, minifying, and concatenating the JavaScript files.

Of course, we're not dependent on Grunt to accomplish this. The LESS compiler we've used in the previous chapters will continue to do its job just fine. And we can manage the combining, minifying, and concatenating of JavaScript by other means as well. (See *Appendix A, Optimizing Site Assets*.)

At present, we simply want to bring in the styles, scripts, and fonts we've already built in *Chapter 2, Bootstrappin' Your Portfolio*. The simplest, most straightforward way to do this is to swap the Roots assets folder for our own folder of assets.

Swapping design assets

In the exercise files, I've provided a folder named __BOOTSTRAPPIN_PORTFOLIO_ ASSETS, which includes a version of our assets files from *Chapter 2, Bootstrappin' Your Portfolio* with a few modifications.

If you care to look inside this folder, there are a few new touches. I've moved the `favicon.ico` and `apple-touch-icon-precomposed.png` files from the `main` folder to their own `ico` folder. Most importantly, I've optimized and compressed the CSS and JavaScript files `main.css`, `main.js`, and `plugins.js` in the steps outlined in *Appendix A*, *Optimizing Site Assets*.

Inside the `__BOOTSTRAPPIN_PORTFOLIO_ASSETS` folder, you'll now see this structure. I've highlighted the files that will be directly linked to our theme as shown in the following screenshot:

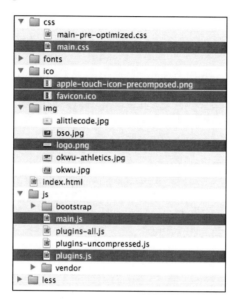

The easiest way to move forward is to move boldly. Let's swap folders:

1. Rename Roots's `assets` folder to `__ROOTS-ASSETS-ORIGINAL`.

2. Rename `__BOOTSTRAPPIN_PORTFOLIO_ASSETS` to `assets`.

3. Now, bear in mind, we will need to update the links to our CSS and JavaScript files, as the Roots' file-naming scheme is slightly different from ours.

4. So, refresh your site, and you should see everything broken, that is, the results of our markup with no stylesheet.

Let's connect our stylesheet!

Connecting our stylesheet

We want to update Roots to use our `main.css` stylesheet. For this, perform the following steps:

1. If you view source on your WordPress site and look for the stylesheet link, you'll see that our path is correct, but that the Roots stylesheet was named `main.min.css` with a version number added. Thus, the path in my locally installed version of WordPress looks like the following path:

   ```
   <link rel="stylesheet" href="http://localhost:8888/bootstrappin-
   portfolio/assets/css/main.min.css?ver=9a2dd99b82ca338b034e8730b
   94139d2">
   ```

> The Roots Gruntfile generates the version number using an MD5 hash. (See the documentation on this at `http://roots.io/using-grunt-for-wordpress-theme-development/`.) This workflow, while a great one, is beyond the scope of this book. We won't be generating a version number for our file.

2. We simply need to update this link to point to our `main.css` file.

3. Roots manages links to stylesheets and scripts using a file in its `lib` folder called `scripts.php`.

4. Open `scripts.php` in your editor.

5. Edit the `enqueue` script lines early in the file. Initially, it reads as the following line of code:

   ```
   wp_enqueue_style('roots_main', get_template_directory_uri()
     . '/assets/css/main.min.css', false,
     '9a2dd99b82ca338b034e8730b94139d2');
   ```

   When done, our updated line should read as the following line of code:

   ```
   wp_enqueue_style('roots_main', get_template_directory_uri()
     . '/assets/css/main.css', false, null);
   ```

6.   Save the changes. Refresh to see if the changes took effect. You should see our custom styles back in place as well as our Font Awesome icons as shown in the following screenshot:

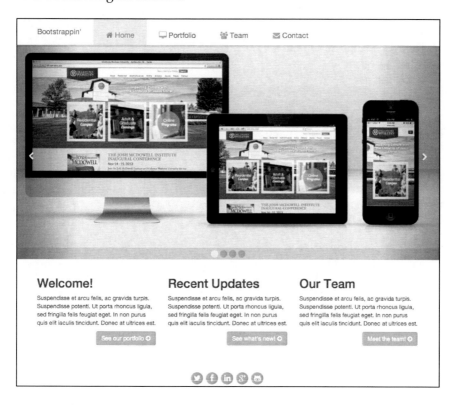

Pause. Enjoy!

But, you may notice that the carousel isn't running. Nor does the responsive navigation button work. We need to connect our JavaScript files.

Connecting our JavaScript files

Roots manages JavaScript links in the same file as the stylesheet link.

So, with `scripts.php` open in your editor, first, we'll check to make sure that our jQuery local fallback is connecting as it should be:

1.   Look for the following lines, which are midway down the `scripts.php` file in the `lib` folder:

```
if ($add_jquery_fallback) {
  echo '<script>window.jQuery || document.write(\'<script
```

```
    src="' . get_template_directory_uri() .
    '/assets/js/vendor/jquery-
    1.10.2.min.js"><\/script>\')</script>' . "\n";
  $add_jquery_fallback = false;
}
```

2. We need to check and make sure that this path and filename matches our
    path and filename:

    `/assets/js/vendor/jquery-1.10.2.min.js`

    As of this writing, and in the exercise files folder `03_Code_BEGIN`, the version
    of the HTML5 Boilerplate used in *Chapter 2, Bootstrappin' Your Portfolio,* is in
    sync with the Roots theme, so the files match.

    If you need to reconcile different versions of jQuery, you'll want to update
    the filename here *and also* update the Google CDN link, which is there earlier
    in the file in the following lines of code:

    ```
    if (!is_admin() && current_theme_supports('jquery-cdn')) {
      wp_deregister_script('jquery');
      wp_register_script('jquery',
        '//ajax.googleapis.com/ajax/libs/jquery/1.10.2/jquery.min.js',
        false, null, false);
    ```

3. Next, we need to double-check our link to the Modernizr script.

 Recall from *Chapter 1, Getting Started with Bootstrap,* that this
script adds HTML5 support for the Internet Explorer 8, among
other good and useful things, such as updating our HTML tag
classes, so we really do want it to work.

You'll find the link to Modernizr in the top section of the file within the
`roots_scripts()` function:

```
wp_register_script('modernizr', get_template_directory_uri() .
  '/assets/js/vendor/modernizr-2.6.2.min.js', false, null,
  false);
```

You simply need to check to ensure that the path and the filename/version
match. Again, the files I've used and have provided in the exercise files
match. In your case, update as needed.

4. Finally, we need to create links to our `plugins.js` and `main.js` files and unhook the Roots equivalent. We'll do this in reverse order shown as follows:

   ○ Start editing the `scripts.php` file in the `lib` folder.

   ○ Roots combines plugins and custom scripts together in one file and registers that script using the following line of code:

```
wp_register_script('roots_scripts',
   get_template_directory_uri() .
   '/assets/js/scripts.min.js', false,
   '2a3e700c4c6e3d70a95b00241a845695', true);
```

We need to comment out or remove that line, so do that now.

   ○ Then, also remove the corresponding line, just a few lines after the previous line of code:

```
wp_enqueue_script('roots_scripts');
```

   ○ Now, we'll register our two script files as shown in the following lines of code:

```
wp_register_script('plugins_script',
   get_template_directory_uri() . '/assets/js/plugins.js',
   false, null, true);
wp_register_script('main_script',
   get_template_directory_uri() . '/assets/js/main.js',
   false, null, true);
```

   ○ Then, we'll enqueue them with the following lines of code:

```
wp_enqueue_script('plugins_script');
wp_enqueue_script('main_script');
```

   ○ Save it and then refresh the page in your browser.

View source and you should see the following lines of code appear (replacing the original) just after the footer tag and before the closing body tag (with the full URL varying depending on the location of your installation):

```
</footer>
<script type='text/javascript'
   src='http://localhost:8888/bootstrappin-
   portfolio/assets/js/plugins.js'></script>
<script type='text/javascript'
   src='http://localhost:8888/bootstrappin-
   portfolio/assets/js/main.js'></script>
</body>
</html>
```

Test the carousel, and it should work.

Test the responsive navbar. It should collapse and gain its drop-down button at narrow window width. The button should expand and then collapse the navbar as designed!

Now let's add our logo image both to the navbar and to the footer.

Adding logo images to the navbar and footer

Let's start by placing the markup for our logo image within the navbar-brand link. We'll find the markup for this in the `header-top-navbar.php` file in the `templates` folder:

1. Open the `header-top-navbar.php` file inside the `templates` folder in your editor.

2. Find the following element:

   ```
   <a class="navbar-brand" ...
   ```

3. Delete the following tag, which places our site name within the navbar brand link:

   ```
   <?php bloginfo('name'); ?>
   ```

4. Replace the previous line of code with the appropriate tag for our logo image:

   ```
   <img src="<?php echo get_template_directory_uri(); ?>/assets/img/logo.png" width="120" alt="Bootstrappin'">
   ```

    Remember that the logo image is built large so that it appears crisp in a retina display. So, be sure to include the `width` attribute. Otherwise, it will appear much too large.

5. Save your results.

6. If you refresh your page, you should see the logo image appear as shown in the following screenshot:

Now for the footer.

Our social icons should be working. The default Roots copyright line will be below them. Let's remove that—at least for the purposes of these exercise files—and place our site logo above the icons.

We'll do this in the footer template file as shown in the following steps:

1. Open the `footer.php` file in the template folder in your editor.

2. I'll remove the following line of code as these exercise files aren't copyrighted:

   ```
   <p>&copy; <?php echo date('Y'); ?> <?php bloginfo('name');
      ?></p>
   ```

3. Then, create a new line above the dynamic sidebar as follows:

   ```
   [NEW LINE HERE ...]
   <?php dynamic_sidebar('sidebar-footer'); ?>
   ```

4. And add a link for our site logo as follows:

   ```
   <p><a href="<?php echo home_url(); ?>/"><img src="<?php
      echo get_template_directory_uri();
      ?>/assets/img/logo.png" width="80"
      alt="Bootstrappin'"></a></p>
   ```

 As in the navbar, be sure here to include the `width` attribute; otherwise, the image will be much too large.

We've employed the WordPress template tags for the `home_url` link and for the `templates` folder. I've wrapped it in a paragraph, but you could choose another element if desired.

5. Save the file. Refresh your browser and you should see the following screenshot:

Our design is nearly complete. But let's not forget our favicon and touch icon.

Adding icon links

To make our theme more easily portable, we need to add links for the `favicon.ico` and `apple-touch-icon-precomposed.png` files in the `head.php` template file:

1. Open the `head.php` file in the `templates` folder.

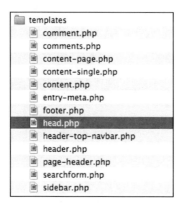

2. Add links to our `favicon.ico` and `apple-touch-icon-precomposed.png` files using the WordPress PHP function `get_template_directory_uri()` to begin the file path. Then, reach into our `ico` folder inside the `assets` folder for the files shown as follows:

```
<!-- Icons -->
<link rel="shortcut icon" href="<?php echo
  get_template_directory_uri(); ?>/assets/ico/favicon.ico">
<link rel="apple-touch-icon-precomposed" href="<?php
  echo get_template_directory_uri(); ?>/assets/ico/apple-
  touch-icon-precomposed.png">
```

3. Save and refresh the file, and depending on your browser's behavior, you should see your favicon appear.

   Here is the screenshot of my resulting favicon in the Google Chrome browser:

Now we just need to attend to a couple of last details to address the specific needs of a WordPress theme.

Adding back WordPress-specific styles

There is a reason we saved the original Roots assets in the __ROOTS_ASSETS_ORIGINAL folder. Though we have everything we need for our design, Roots included two key sets of WordPress-specific styles that we lack and may want to bring back in.

First, in the original Roots CSS folder, you'll find the editor-style.css file. As this file enables us to improve the WYSIWYG editing experience, we may want to copy this file to our own CSS folder. (You could also opt to create your own custom version of this file to more closely match your custom styles.)

Second, if we intend to have a blog in our site or to distribute our theme, we'll want to recover a few key styles specific to WordPress, which Roots has provided us in the app.less file in the less folder. It is only a small matter to add these to our own custom LESS file and then recompile into our main.css file. To add WordPress-specific styles, perform the following steps:

1. Open the Roots app.less file inside the less folder in your editor.

2. In another editor window, create a new file named _wp.less and save it within our own custom assets in the less folder as shown in the following screenshot:

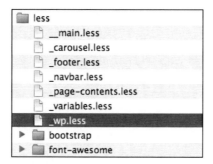

3. Copy the following lines of code from app.less to _wp.less as they ensure we address WordPress-generated classes for images:

```
/* =========================
   WordPress Generated Classes
   . . .
   ========================= */

aligncenter { display: block; margin: 0 auto; }
alignleft { float: left; }
alignright { float: right; }
figure.alignnone { margin-left: 0; margin-right: 0; }
```

4. If you anticipate running a blog in your WordPress site, you'll also want to speed up your blog design process by adding the section of selectors for posts. The selectors found here cover the elements and class names used in the Roots template for blog posts.

```
/* =======================
    Posts
    ======================= */

hentry header { }
hentry time { }
hentry .byline { }
hentry .entry-content { }
hentry footer { }
```

5. If you anticipate using a sidebar in a section of your site, grab the `.sidebar` selector.

6. You may want to pull over other selectors as reminders of the classes that Roots uses by default: `.content`, `.main`, `.sidebar`, and so on.

7. Also note the styles used for gallery shortcode:

```
/* Gallery Shortcode */
.gallery-row { padding: 15px 0; }
```

8. After bringing over the lines you'd like to keep, take a few moments to convert comments from block comments to single-line comments so that they will not compile to CSS.

```
//      Posts
//      -----------------------
...


//      WordPress Generated Classes
//      -----------------------
```

9. Save `_wp.less`.

10. Close `app.less`.

11. Now open `__main.less` and add a line to import `_wp.less` as shown in the following lines of code:

```
// Other custom files
@import "_page-contents.less";
@import "_footer.less";
@import "_wp.less";
```

12. Recompile `__main.less` to `css/main.css` — being sure to minify the CSS output to ensure best performance.

That's it! Not only have we integrated our custom design, but we've prepared our theme for whatever we may need to do next with WordPress.

Summary

Let's review what we've done:

- We began with the excellent Roots theme as our starter theme for WordPress
- We've asserted control over the markup structure by customizing the following template files:
    - `head.php`: This is used to add favicon and touch icon links
    - `header-top-navbar.php`: This is used to add our logo image
    - `footer.php`: This is used to add our logo image
- We've created the following custom template files:
    - `page-home.php` — from `template-custom.php`
    - `base-page-home.php` — from `base.php`
    - `content-home.php` — from `content-page.php`
- We've utilized custom fields to manage the content of our complex home page
- We've leveraged a footer widget to put our social media icons in place
- We've integrated our own custom-compiled assets — our LESS, CSS, and JavaScript
- To integrate our custom design assets, we've edited Roots' `scripts.php` file to update links to our CSS and JavaScript files
- And we've brought back in from Roots a set of styles helpful for addressing details of a WordPress website

Congratulations! That's quite an accomplishment.

The process we've used in this chapter can be used to transform any Bootstrap design into a WordPress theme.

So, let's turn back to designing with Bootstrap. Next, we are going to design a business site.

4
Bootstrappin' Business

We've built our portfolio site and converted it to a WordPress theme. Now, it's time to flesh out our portfolio with some projects that demonstrate the range of our powers. Let's now turn to designing a complex business home page.

Take a moment to survey the home pages of successful businesses, such as these:

- Zappos (http://zappos.com)
- Amazon (http://amazon.com)
- Adobe (http://adobe.com)
- HP (http://hp.com)

While each has its own approach, what these sites have in common is that they manage considerable complexity.

We can get a grasp of some common features by breaking the website down into three categories, as follows, based on regions of the page:

- **Banner/Masthead**: This part contains the logo, main navigation with dropdowns, a secondary or utility navigation, and a login or register option
- **Main content area**: This features a complex layout with at least three columns, if not more
- **Footer**: This is filled with multiple columns of links and information

Let's demonstrate our ability to manage this degree of complexity. To do so, we will take full advantage of Bootstrap's responsive 12-column grid system.

Here is the design we'll create, when viewed in medium and wide viewports:

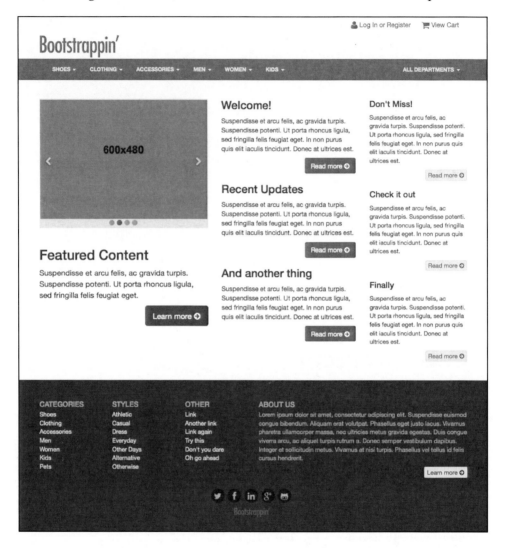

In narrow viewports, it will adapt considerably, as shown in the following screenshot:

After that, we will perform the following steps:

1. Begin with a set of starter files based on the Portfolio project from *Chapter 2, Bootstrappin' Your Portfolio*.
2. Create a complex banner with the logo above the navbar and a utility navigation in the far top-right corner—in desktop viewports.
3. For smaller viewports, we'll enable our utility options to appear only as icons atop the collapsed responsive navbar.
4. Implement a business-style color scheme.
5. Make adjustments to both the responsive and desktop versions of the navbar.
6. Set up complex multicolumn grids for the main content and footer areas.

First things first. Let's size up our project starter files.

Sizing up our beginning files

As with all the projects in this book, the beginning files for this project be downloaded from the Packt Publishing website at `http://www.packtpub.com/support`. You'll find the files for this project in the folder `04_Code_BEGIN`.

These files are based largely on our results from *Chapter 2, Bootstrappin' Your Portfolio*. Thus, we have the benefit of these key components:

- Bootstrap LESS and JavaScript files, which have been organized in the following directories:
  - `less/bootstrap`: This contains Bootstrap's LESS files
  - `js/bootstrap`: This contains Bootstrap's individual plugins
  - `js/plugins.js`: This contains all Bootstrap plugins in minified form

- The HTML5 Boilerplate along with the following files:
  - The basic markup structure of `index.html`
  - `js/vendor/modernizr-2.6.2.min.js`
  - `js/vendor/query-1.10.2.min.js`

- The `respond.js` file for Internet Explorer 8 compatibility:
  - `js/vendor/respond.js`

- Font Awesome font icons, including the following:
  - Icon fonts in the `fonts` directory
  - LESS files in the `less/font-awesome` directory

In addition to these key assets, we have some of the custom LESS touches we created during the project in *Chapter 2, Bootstrappin' Your Portfolio*. They can be found in the following files that are present in the `less` directory:

- `__main.less`: This is based on `bootstrap.less`, customized to import Bootstrap's LESS files from the `less/bootstrap` directory as well as Font Awesome font icons and our custom LESS files
- `_carousel.less`: This is based on Bootstrap's `carousel.less` file and has custom touches on the carousel padding, background, and indicators
- `_footer.less`: This contains styles for the layout and design of the logo and social icons

- `_navbar.less`: It is based on Bootstrap's `navbar.less` file and has adjusted padding in the `.navbar-brand` class to enable the navbar logo to fit

- `_page-contents.less`: It contains styles to ensure that columns with floated buttons clear one another in narrow single-column layouts

- `_variables.less`: It is based on Bootstrap's `variables.less` file and has custom versions of gray and some adjustments to variables for the navbar and carousel

> If desired, you could choose to follow the steps for this exercise with a fresh download of Bootstrap's assets. You'll simply need to use Glyphicons rather than Font Awesome icons. You'll lack the custom styles from these files, but you can adjust and adapt your own approach.
>
> I've sought to indicate the customizations I've made to files copied from Bootstrap with single-line comments—commenting out a line or adding comments such as `// edited` or `// added`.

Next, let's examine the content provided in the `index.html` file, as I've set it up to give us a running start. Open it in your browser, and you should see this in desktop width:

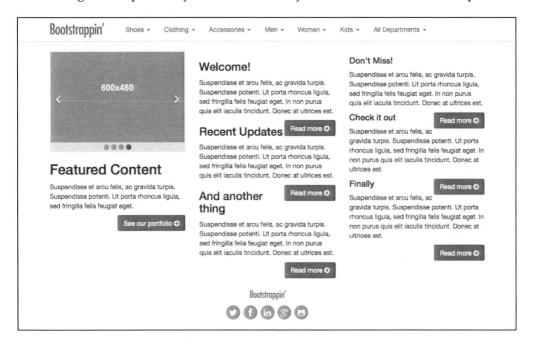

Note the following features:

- A complex navbar that has seven main `nav` items, each with a dropdown
- The first of the three columns is equipped with a carousel, followed by a heading, paragraph, and button
- The second and third columns that have headings, paragraphs, and **Read more ->** buttons
- A footer that has the logo and social icons

You'll recognize elements we've already worked with in *Chapter 2, Bootstrappin' Your Portfolio*. The carousel is now smaller—constrained by its containing column. Otherwise, the markup is the same.

One wrinkle is that I've used the excellent `holder.js` JavaScript plugin to dynamically generate placeholder images for our carousel. If you examine the markup, you'll see near the bottom of the page that I've included the `holder.js` script right before `plugins.js`, as follows:

```
<!-- Holder.js for project development only -->
<script src="js/vendor/holder.js"></script>
```

We won't be using placeholder images in our final production site, so it makes sense to link it separately with a prominent comment.

With `holder.js` in place, we can conveniently build image tags that reference `holder.js` as their source. The remainder of the pseudo-URL specifies dimensions, color, and filler text, as follows:

```
<img src="holder.js/600x480/auto/vine/textmode:literal"
  alt="Holder Image">
```

For more information about `holder.js`, consult the documentation at `https://github.com/imsky/holder`.

With these elements in place—and thanks in particular to Bootstrap's ready repertoire of styles and behaviors—we're starting out in good shape. Let's get to the details.

First, we'll reposition our navbar within a more complex banner design.

Creating a complex banner area

Let's start from the top and create our complex banner area with the following features:

- A site logo positioned above the navbar for desktops and larger viewports
- A navbar with many menu items, including dropdowns
- A utility navigation area
- A login form with username and password
- An option to register

Here is the mockup of our desired end goal on a desktop-width viewport:

On a narrow viewport, it will adjust to this:

We'll start by working on a new arrangement for our top logo.

Placing a logo above the navbar

In this new design, we need a logo in two spots, for two contexts:

- For desktop and widescreen viewports, we want the logo to display above the navbar
- For tablet and phone viewports, we want the logo to display within the responsive navbar

Thanks to Bootstrap's responsive utility classes, we can do both! Here's how:

1. Open `index.html` in your editor.
2. From the navbar, copy the `navbar-brand` link and image. It looks like this:

   ```
   <a class="navbar-brand" href="index.html"><img src=
     "img/logo.png" alt="Bootstrappin'" width="120"></a>
   ```

3. Paste a copy of it up above, just after the `<header role="banner">` tag and before `<nav role="navigation" class="navbar navbar-default">`.

4. Wrap the logo with `<div class="container">...</div>` to constrain it within Bootstrap's centered grid space.

5. Edit the class on your new logo link, so that it reads `banner-brand` rather than `navbar-brand`. And let's change the image width attribute to `180`.

 Recall that our original logo image is large, about 900px wide. We've resized it to 120px wide via the `width` attribute (we could alternatively use CSS rules) in order to pack its pixels tighter for retina screens.

The resulting code should look like this:

```
<header role="banner">
  <div class="container">
    <a class="banner-brand" href="index.html"><img src="img/logo.png"
alt="Bootstrappin'" width="180"></a>
  </div><!-- /.container -->
  <nav role="navigation" class="navbar navbar-default">
```

Save the changes and refresh the page in your browser. You should see the new copy of the logo above the navbar.

Now let's adjust our logos so that they are displayed only when needed.

In `_variables.less`, we need to double-check the value of the `@grid-float-breakpoint` variable. You'll find it by searching for the variable name. This value is set as follows in the default `less/bootstrap/variables.less` file:

```
// Point at which the navbar stops collapsing
@grid-float-breakpoint:    @screen-sm-min;
```

This variable determines the point at which the navbar collapses for narrower viewports and expands for wider viewports. In our case, given the complexity of our navigation, we need to ensure that the navbar collapses at the next, larger breakpoint. Therefore, we need to ensure our variable is set at the `@screen-md-min` breakpoint. If you began with the `04_Code_BEGIN` files, you should see this already set as follows. (If not, you'll need to update it.)

```
// Point at which the navbar stops collapsing
@grid-float-breakpoint:     @screen-md-min;
```

With this variable set appropriately, we now want the `banner-brand` class to display for medium and large viewports only and `navbar-brand` to display only for small and extra-small viewports. Bootstrap provides a set of helpful responsive utility classes to address just this need. You can see the documentation on these classes at `http://getbootstrap.com/css/#responsive-utilities`.

Let's put them to use for our purposes:

1. Add the class `visible-md visible-lg` to the `banner-brand` class:

    ```
    <a class="banner-brand visible-md visible-lg"
      href="index.html"><img src="img/logo.png"
      alt="Bootstrappin'" width="180"></a>
    ```

2. Add the class `visible-xs visible-sm` to the `navbar-brand` class:

    ```
    <a class="navbar-brand visible-xs visible-sm"
      href="index.html"><img src="img/logo.png"
      alt="Bootstrappin'" width="120"></a>
    ```

Save the changes and refresh the page, and you should see these results! In medium and large viewports, only the `banner-brand` class will appear:

In small and extra-small viewports, only the `navbar-brand` will appear:

Ah, the beauty of Bootstrap!

> If you are concerned about having both sets of tags for these alternately hidden logo images cluttering up your markup, it is possible to get the same result with a bit of JavaScript work to swap out the elements as needed.
>
> An advantage of the current approach, however, is that it does not rely upon JavaScript. It doesn't slow page loading times either, since we are using the same image in both places and require no new HTTP requests. All in all, our current approach is a credible, defensible solution; in addition to being easy to implement.

Now, let's make some adjustments to our navbar.

Reviewing and checking navbar dropdown items

The navbar, with its seven items and submenus, reflects the needs of a large complex website.

The markup for the dropdown menus is taken directly from the Bootstrap navbar documentation at `http://getbootstrap.com/components/#navbar`.

If you look at our resulting markup, you'll notice these special classes and attributes:

- `class="dropdown"` on the parent `li`
- `class="dropdown-toggle"` on the link
- `attribute="data-toggle"` also on the link
- `class="dropdown-menu"` on the submenu `ul` element

Here is the resulting markup:

```
<li class="dropdown">
    <a href="#" class="dropdown-toggle" data-toggle="dropdown">Shoes
      <b class="caret"></b></a>
    <ul class="dropdown-menu">
      <li><a href="#">Action</a></li>
      <li><a href="#">Another action</a></li>
      <li><a href="#">Something else here</a></li>
      ...
    </ul>
</li>
```

Also note the special tag and class used to display a small dropdown indicator:
`<b class="caret"></b>`. (You'll see the CSS used to create this indicator in `less/bootstrap/dropdowns.less`.)

 If you happen to be making use of files from a previous project rather than this chapter's starter files (`04_Code_BEGIN`), you may need to double-check your import lines in `_main.less` to ensure that it imports `bootstrap/dropdowns.less`. Also double-check `plugins.js` to ensure that it includes the plugin `bootstrap-dropdown.js`.

With the LESS, JavaScript, and markup in place, our navbar and its dropdowns should presently look and work as shown in the following screenshot. (Note that Bootstrap dropdowns respond on click.)

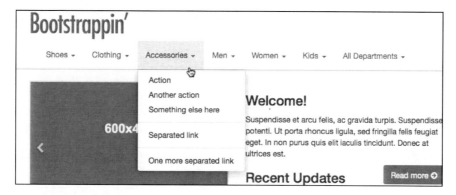

Now that we're familiar with the markup structure and have ensured everything's working as it should, let's move the **All Departments** menu to the right-hand end of the navbar, setting it apart from the others.

To do this, we need to nest this list item within its own unordered list as follows:

1. Before the **All Departments** list item, close the `ul` tag for `ul class="nav"`, which surrounds all previous menu items.

2. Start a new `ul` tag with the classes `nav` and `navbar-nav` before the **All Departments** menu item. Once this opening tag is added, it will nest this list item in the standard structure for navigation menus.

3. In addition to the classes `nav` and `navbar-nav`, add a third class, `pull-right`, which is a convenient Bootstrap utility class, to float an element to the right.

The newly added lines are highlighted in the following snippet—after which I'll include the original list item and link in context:

```
</ul>
<ul class="nav navbar-nav pull-right">
  <li class="dropdown">
  <a href="#" class="dropdown-toggle" data-toggle="dropdown">All
Departments <b class="caret"></b></a>
```

Save the changes and refresh the page, and you should see the **All Departments** drop-down menu item float to the right-hand end of the navbar as follows:

So far so good! Now, let's add our utility navigation.

Adding utility navigation

This project requires utility navigation to allow users to log in or register and to view their carts.

On medium and large viewports, we'll place this utility navigation in the very top-right corner of our banner area as follows:

On smaller screens, we'll display icons at the far right of the collapsed navbar:

Let's set this up.

Still working in `index.html`, we need to add the markup for our utility navigation within the banner, just after the `banner-brand` attribute. Here is the full markup, beginning with the opening `header` tag for our banner area. I've highlighted the new `utility-nav` markup in the following code snippet:

```
<header role="banner">
  <div class="container">
    <a class="banner-brand visible-md visible-lg" href=
      "index.html"><img src="img/logo.png" alt="Bootstrappin'"
      width="180"></a>
    <div class="utility-nav">
      <ul>
        <li><a href="#" title="Login or Register"><i class="icon
          fa fa-user fa-lg"></i> Log In or Register</a></li>
        <li><a href="#" title="View Cart"><i class="icon fa fa-
          shopping-cart fa-lg"></i> View Cart</a></li>
      </ul>
    </div><!-- /.utility-nav -->
  </div><!-- /.container -->
```

Note a few things about this markup:

- The class `utility-nav` is simply created for our use. It is not a Bootstrap specific class and has no specific styles attached.

- I've included Font Awesome's user and shopping cart icons and added the class of `fa-lg` to increase their size by 33 percent. See Font Awesome's documentation on this at `http://fontawesome.io/examples/#larger`.

Save the changes and refresh the page, and you should see our new `utility-nav` class appear just below the `banner-brand` logo as follows:

Now, to complete the layout and related adjustments, we need to apply some custom styles. We need a new file to manage styles for our banner area. This can be accomplished as follows:

1. Create a new file, `_banner.less`, and save it directly within the `less` folder, alongside our other custom LESS files.

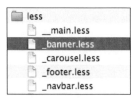

2. Add `_banner.less` to the import sequence in `__main.less`.

   ```
   // Other custom files
   @import "_banner.less"; // added
   ```

3. In `_banner.less`, provide a helpful comment at the top. We need to set the position of `.utility-nav` to absolute, at the top right. We'll specify `header[role="banner"]` as the context for these styles.

   ```
   //// Banner Area Styles
   //
   header[role="banner"] {
     .utility-nav {
       position: absolute;
       top: 0;
       right: 0;
     }
   }
   ```

4. Now, let's refine the details as follows:

   1. Increase the height of our banner area by adding top padding to the `.banner-brand` class.

   2. Set the positioning of the banner `container` to `relative` so that it will contain our absolute-positioned `utility-nav` class.

   3. Remove bullets from the unordered list.

   4. Float the list items on the left.

   5. Display the `inline-block` links and add padding.

   6. Remove underlines from the hover effect.

The following lines will accomplish these goals:

```
header[role="banner"] {
  .banner-brand {
    padding-top: 40px;
  }
  > .container {
    position: relative;
  }
  .utility-nav {
    position: absolute;
    top: 0;
    right: 0;
    > ul {
      list-style: none;
      > li {
        float: left;
        > a {
          display: inline-block;
          padding: 8px 12px;
          &:hover {
            text-decoration: none;
          }
        }
      }
    }
  }
}
```

Save the changes and ensure that it compiles. Make sure your browser window is at desktop width. Refresh it. You should see your utility-nav class take its place at the top right of the banner:

That takes care of medium viewports and larger. Now, let's address the needs of the collapsed responsive navbar.

Making responsive adjustments

Our `utility-nav` class runs into problems when the navbar collapses for small screens. The most immediate problem is that it disappears:

We can make our `utility-nav` class visible again by assigning it a `z-index` value greater than that of the navbar's, which is set to `1000` by a variable in `_variables.less`. In `_banner.less`, set the `z-index` property of `.utility-nav` to `1999`.

```
.utility-nav {
  ...
  z-index: 1999;
```

This will bring our utility navigation back to the foreground as seen in the following screenshot:

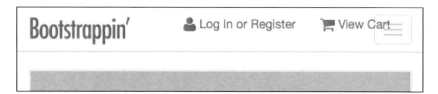

Now the problem is that it overlaps our `navbar-toggle` button. We need to move the toggle to the left side of our navbar. This can be done as follows:

1. Open `less/_navbar.less` in your editor.

2. Search for the comment `// Navbar toggle`. We'll edit the lines within the `.navbar-toggle` selector immediately beneath this comment, changing the `float` value from `right` to `left` and `margin-right` to `margin-left`:

```
.navbar-toggle {
  position: relative;
  float: left; // edited
  margin-left: @navbar-padding-horizontal; // edited
```

Save and compile these changes, and you'll see the navbar toggle shift to the left end of the collapsed navbar, as shown in the following screenshot:

So far so good.

Now to address the problem of crowding by hiding the text for all devices except for screen readers on the collapsed navbar. In an uncluttered collapsed navbar, the icons will be enough to communicate the point, especially if we make the icons larger. Let's do that:

1. In `index.html`, place `span` tags around the text within each link of our `utility-nav` class as follows:

    ```
    <li><a href="#" title="Login or Register"><i class="icon fa
       fa-user fa-lg"></i> <span>Log In or
       Register</span></a></li>
    <li><a href="#" title="View Cart"><i class="icon fa
       fa-shopping-cart fa-lg"></i> <span>
       View Cart</span></a></li>
    ```

    This will give us a handle for our upcoming style adjustment.

2. Now, in `_banner.less`, we'll add a media query to target these `span` tags. Thanks to the power of LESS, we can nest the media query precisely where we want it to do its work. We'll use the `@grid-float-breakpoint` variable, setting a `max-width` query to the `@grid-float-breakpoint` value minus one, since this variable determines the point at which our navbar makes the transition from collapsed to expanded. Within this media query, we'll use the utility class `sr-only` as a mixin to hide text from all devices except screen readers. (See the documentation on this class at `http://getbootstrap.com/css/#helper-classes-screen-readers`.) Here is the code snippet:

    ```
    .utility-nav {
       . . .
       . . .
       > a {
          . . .
    ```

```
@media (max-width: (@grid-float-breakpoint - 1)) {
  span {
  .sr-only();
  }
 }
 }
}
```

This will hide the text between our span tags, leaving us only with the icons!

3. Now, we will increase the size of the icons and add some line height to position them vertically. We'll do this within the same media query:

```
@media (max-width: @grid-float-breakpoint) {
  span {
    .sr-only();
  }
  .icon {
    font-size: 2em;
    line-height: 1.2;
  }
}
```

Save, compile, and refresh; you should see the following result:

Take a minute to resize your browser window back and forth across the breakpoint. You should see the entire banner and navbar adjust seamlessly across the breakpoint.

If you're like me, it's hard not to be pleased with a framework that enables us to be this efficient at building such an adept and responsive interface.

Next up, we need to begin implementing the color scheme.

Implementing the color scheme

We've been provided with a business-friendly palette of blue, red, and gray. Let's work these colors into our color variables:

1. Open `_variables.less` in your editor. We'll be working at the beginning of the file, in the color variables.

2. Let's review the range of grays we have available. If you've begun with the `04_Code_BEGIN` files, you'll see we've carried these variables over from *Chapter 2, Bootstrappin' Your Portfolio*. They served us well there, and we'll make use of them again here.

   ```
   // Grays
   // -----------------------

   @gray-darker:           #222; // edited
   @gray-dark:             #454545; // edited
   @gray:                  #777; // edited
   @gray-light:            #aeaeae; // edited
   @gray-lighter:          #ccc; // edited
   @gray-lightest:         #ededed; // edited
   @off-white:             #fafafa; // edited
   ```

3. Now, below the grays, let's fold in our new brand colors. We'll modify the value for `@brand-primary` and create an `@brand-feature` variable for red:

   ```
   @brand-primary:         #3e7dbd; // edited blue
   @brand-feature:         #c60004; // added new red
   ```

4. Now, let's adjust our link hover color so that it will lighten (rather than darken) the `@brand-primary` color, which is already dark:

   ```
   // Links
   // -----------------------
   @link-color:            @brand-primary;
   @link-color-hover:      lighten(@link-color, 15%);
   ```

Having set up these fundamental color variables, we're ready to work on our navbar.

Styling the collapsed navbar

While still in `_navbar.less`, search for `// Navbar`, which will take you to the navbar variables. Note that most of the standard values specified here will affect both the collapsed responsive navbar for small viewports and the expanded navbar for wider viewports.

We want the background, text, and link colors for the collapsed responsive navbar to remain largely consistent with the default values but then change to our blue background and a light text color for medium and larger viewports.

Let's check and adjust a few values for the default variables and then create a new set of variables to apply only to the expanded navbar, as follows:

1. Reduce the value of `@navbar-height` to `44px`, and then apply the variables we set earlier where they fit here. Change `@navbar-default-color` to `@text-color` and `@navbar-default-bg` to `@white`.

    ```less
    // Basics of a navbar
    @navbar-height:                     44px;
    ...
    @navbar-default-color:              @text-color;
    @navbar-default-bg:                 #fff;
    ```

2. Moving on down to the navbar links section, make these adjustments, which will make links consistent with navbar text and give active links a slight background color adjustment:

    ```less
    // Navbar links
    @navbar-default-link-color:         @navbar-default-color;
    @navbar-default-link-hover-color:   @navbar-default-color;
    @navbar-default-link-hover-bg:      darken
      (@navbar-default-bg, 5%);
    @navbar-default-link-active-color:  @navbar-default-color;
    @navbar-default-link-active-bg:     @navbar-default-link-
      hover-bg;
    ```

3. Next, let's adjust the styling of `navbar-toggle`, removing the border and background and darkening the bars:

    ```less
    // Navbar toggle
    @navbar-default-toggle-hover-bg:        transparent;
    @navbar-default-toggle-icon-bar-bg:     @gray;
    @navbar-default-toggle-border-color:    transparent;
    ```

Save, compile, and refresh the browser, and you should see the following result for the collapsed navbar in narrow viewports:

We have just two features of our collapsed navbar to refine. If you toggle the collapsed navbar's dropdown behavior, you'll notice that the **All Departments** link floats to the right.

Recall that we placed a `pull-right` class on the **All Departments** menu item, to float it to the right on the expanded navbar. In this context, however, we'd like it to remain to the left. Bootstrap has a class for this! Let's make the switch.

In `index.html`, find the lines for the **All Departments** markup and exchange the class `pull-right` for `navbar-right`, as follows:

```
<ul class="nav navbar-nav navbar-right">
   <li class="dropdown">
      <a href="#" class="dropdown-toggle" data-toggle="dropdown">All
Departments <b class="caret"></b></a>
```

If you'd like to see how this works, open `_navbar.less` and search for `.navbar-right`. You'll find these lines with an explanatory comment above them:

```
@media (min-width: @grid-float-breakpoint) {
   .navbar-left  { .pull-left(); }
   .navbar-right { .pull-right(); }
}
```

Nested within a media query which applies only to the expanded navbar, these classes were created exactly for cases such as ours. After applying the new `navbar-right` class, save `index.html`, refresh it, and you'll see **All Departments** float to the left in the collapsed navbar while still floating to the right on the expanded navbar.

Outstanding! Now, let's adjust the behavior of the drop-down menus within the navbar. As of Bootstrap 3.0.2, the drop-down menu items are configured as `full-width` within the collapsed navbar—but only when the navbar collapses at the original `@grid-float-breakpoint` value of `@screen-sm-min`. Because we've adjusted this value to `@screen-md-min`, our dropdowns no longer fill the full width. You can test this by setting your browser window to the `@screen-sm` range (768-991px) and trying the drop-down menu behavior.

You'll see this happen:

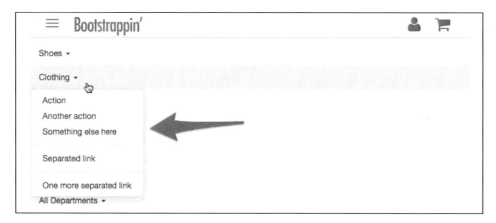

We can fix this to behave as it should by adjusting one media query:

1. Open `_navbar.less` and search for `.open.dropdown-menu`. You will notice that it's nested within a media query, like so:

   ```
   @media (max-width: @screen-xs-max) {
     // Dropdowns get custom display when collapsed
     .open.dropdown-menu {
   ```

2. We need to adjust this media query so that its `max-width` value is the same as the value of `@grid-float-breakpoint`. In fact, let's simply use that variable itself, so that they will always correspond:

   ```
   @media (max-width: @grid-float-breakpoint) {
   ```

Save the changes, compile the file, and refresh the page, and you should see that the drop-down menus now expand to their full width:

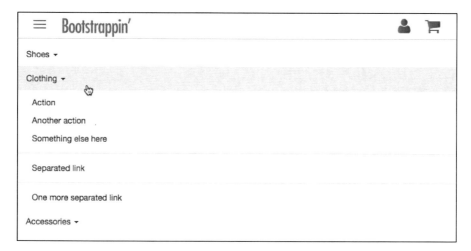

Fantastic. Now we can address the horizontal navbar.

Styling the horizontal navbar

For medium and large viewports—where our navbar stretches out horizontally below the logo—we want our navbar to take on the blue color we've set up as our @brand-primary variable. This will require us to invert the colors of links and text from dark to light. We'll use Bootstrap's inverted-navbar variables and styles to accomplish this as follows:

1. In _variables.less, search for the comment // Inverted navbar. There, you'll find variables much like those for the default navbar. We'll use these to apply the desired colors for our expanded navbar.

2. Adjust these variables as follows:

    ```
    // Inverted navbar
    //
    // Reset inverted navbar basics
    @navbar-inverse-color:              @gray-lightest;
    @navbar-inverse-bg:                 @brand-primary;
    @navbar-inverse-border:             darken
       (@navbar-inverse-bg, 10%);


    // Inverted navbar links
    @navbar-inverse-link-color:         @navbar-inverse-color;
    @navbar-inverse-link-hover-color:   #fff;
    @navbar-inverse-link-hover-bg:      darken(@navbar-inverse-bg, 5%);
    @navbar-inverse-link-active-color:  @navbar-inverse-link-
       hover-color;
    @navbar-inverse-link-active-bg:     darken
       (@navbar-inverse-bg, 10%);
    ```

    With these variables in place, we only need to apply these styles to the expanded version of the navbar. This requires writing just a few lines of custom LESS. Since this color shift is part of our overall strategy for the banner area, let's add these to our _banner.less file.

3. Open _banner.less and add a new commented section with these lines:

    ```
    // Apply .navbar-inverse styles to the expanded navbar
    @media (min-width: @grid-float-breakpoint) {
      .navbar-default {
        .navbar-inverse();
      }
    }
    ```

This media query uses the @grid-float-breakpoint variable to establish the minimum viewport width at which this new rule applies. Recalling that we've already placed the class navbar-default on our navbar, we can use that class as the selector. The .navbar-inverse() mixin applies the entire battery of .navbar-inverse styles from _navbar.less to our navbar within the context of this media query.

Save these changes, compile the file, and refresh your browser. In medium and large viewport widths, you should see the navbar take on the new blue color and the text turn light!

At this point, you may notice the rounded corners at the ends of our navbar. We want to remove these. This can be done in _variables.less. Search for the variable @navbar-border-radius and set its value to 0:

```
@navbar-border-radius:                0;
```

Finally, let's transform the text to uppercase, reduce its size a bit, and make it bold.

In _banner.less, add these highlighted lines just after the .navbar-inverse() mixin:

```
@media (min-width: @grid-float-breakpoint) {
  .navbar-default {
    .navbar-inverse();
    .navbar-nav > li > a {
      text-transform: uppercase;
      font-size: 82%;
      font-weight: bold;
    }
  }
}
```

This will yield the following result:

Here is a closeup with one item hovered over:

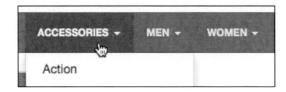

Our banner and navbar are complete! Now it's time to move on to the main content of our page.

Designing a complex responsive layout

Let's imagine we've emerged from client meetings with a plan to organize the home page content in three tiers, ranked by importance.

In medium and wide viewports, this content will be laid out in three columns as seen in the following screenshot:

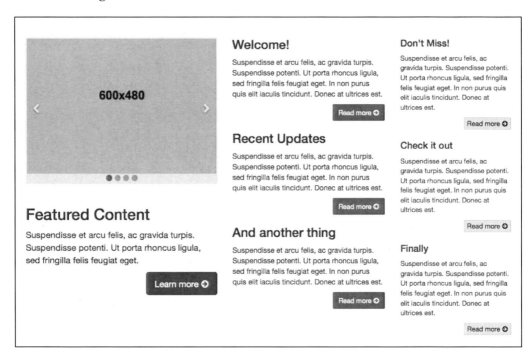

In a narrow viewport, these will be laid out one after another, in a single vertical column:

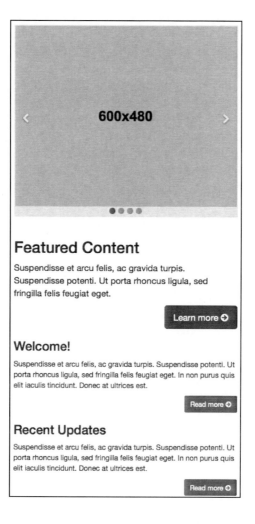

And in a small, `tablet-width` viewport, we'll arrange the content in two side-by-side columns, with the third tier of content laid out beneath it as a horizontal row as seen in the following screenshot:

To get us started, I've provided the basic markup for three equal columns. Let's review what we have and then adapt it to the needs of this design. We'll begin with the three-column layout for medium and wide viewports.

Adjusting the medium and wide layout

Currently, in medium and wide viewports, our three columns are equal in width, font size, and button size and color. As a result, the presentation lacks visual hierarchy, as seen in the following screenshot:

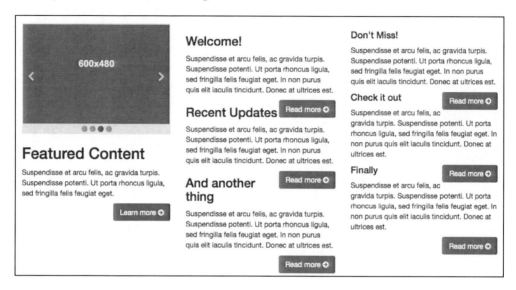

We can take significant strides by adjusting column width, font size, and button size and color to establish a clearer hierarchy between these tiers of content. Let's do that. We'll start by adjusting column widths:

1. In `index.html`, search for the `section` tag for the primary content:

   ```
   <section class="content-primary col-sm-4">
   ```

   Note that the class `col-sm-4` sets the width of this column to one-third of the width of the parent element, beginning at the small viewport width (764px and up).

   We want to save the three-column layout for the medium and large viewports (992px and up), and we want this first column to be wider than the others.

2. Edit the class `col-sm-4` to read `col-md-5`, as follows:

   ```
   <section class="content-primary col-md-5">
   ```

   This will set this column to 5/12 width beginning at the medium viewport and up.

3. Now search and find the opening `section` tags for the next two columns and adjust the column classes to `col-md-4` and `col-md-3` respectively:

```
<section class="content-secondary col-md-4">
...
<section class="content-tertiary col-md-3">
```

Save, refresh, and you'll see the desired visual hierarchy in the width of our columns:

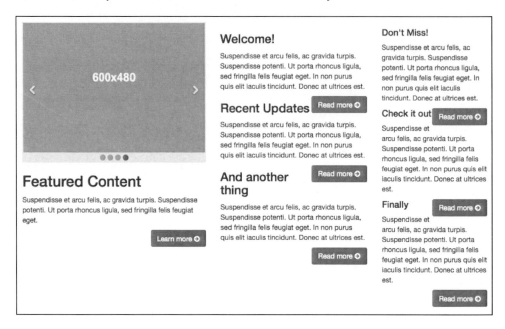

You might have noticed that the headings in the middle of the secondary and tertiary columns are not clearing the buttons above them. Let's adjust these, as well as our buttons and font sizes.

Adjusting headings, font sizes, and buttons

Let's begin by adjusting our headings so that they consistently clear the buttons above them, which have been floated to the right. For this purpose, we'll use the file we previously created to manage the details of the page contents: `_page-contents.less`.

Here's how to do it:

1. In _page-contents.less, let's write a selector to select headings h1 through h4 when they're nested inside a Bootstrap column class. We'll use the CSS2 attribute selector and cover our bases by targeting any element whose classes include the string col-.

     Later in this chapter, we will equip our footer with its own set of responsive columns. Thus, we need to make sure we nest these rules within the selector for the main element.

    Within this context, we'll select all heading tags we might potentially use and set them to clear floated elements, with some added padding for separation.

    ```
    main {
    ...
      [class*="col-"] {
        h1, h2, h3, h4 {
        clear: both;
        padding-top: 20px;
        }
      }
    }
    ```

    This gives the necessary separation between our headings and floated buttons. But it also creates unneeded padding at the top of the secondary and tertiary columns.

    In the following image, the lower arrows highlight the improvement accomplished now that our headings clear the floated buttons. The top arrows highlight the ragged top edge of our columns, where padding causes a problem.

    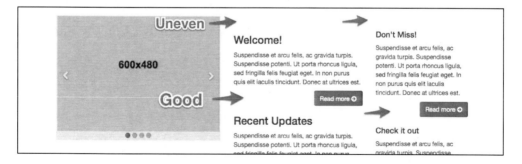

2. Let's remove the margin and padding from the uppermost heading in each column. We'll use the :first-child selector for this, nesting these lines within our heading selectors. We'll use the & combinator, which in this formulation, allows us to select any first-child instance of these headings:

```
h1, h2, h3, h4 {
  ...
  &:first-child {
    margin-top: 0;
    padding-top: 0;
  }
}
```

3. This removes the extra margin and padding and evens up the top edge of our columns as follows:

4. However, we only want to remove this top margin and padding in small or larger viewports, which accommodate multiple columns. Thus, we need to nest this rule within a media query corresponding with the breakpoint at which our layout expands from a narrow single-column layout to a wider multicolumn layout.

Thus, we need to nest what we've just done within a media query for small viewports and up:

```
@media (min-width: @screen-sm-min) {
  &:first-child {
    margin-top: 0;
    padding-top: 0;
  }
}
```

With the preceding media query, we've retained the padding we need between elements in the single-column layout for narrow viewports, as seen in the following screenshot:

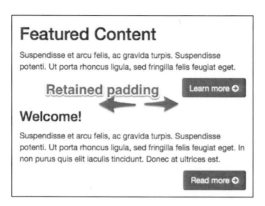

With this accomplished, we can move on to adjust buttons and font sizes to reflect the informational hierarchy of our content. Let's begin by enlarging the font size and button size and color in our primary content area.

Enhancing the primary column

First, let's increase the font size of our primary column content:

1. In _variables.less, search for the @font-size-large variable and update its value to the following:

    ```
    ceil(@font-size-base * 1.15);
    ```

2. Now, in _page-contents.less, add these lines to use this font size for the content of our primary content:

    ```
    .content-primary {
      font-size: @font-size-large;
    }
    ```

Save these changes, compile the file, and refresh your browser. You should see the font size increase accordingly!

Now, let's adjust the color of our button to utilize the red @brand-feature color. We'll utilize the @brand-feature variable we set up in _variables.less.

```
@brand-feature:        #c60004;
```

We'll also utilize an excellent mixin provided in the Bootstrap `mixins.less` file. You may want to take a moment to check it out. Open `bootstrap/mixins.less` and search for `// Button` variants. You'll find a mixin that begins as follows:

```
.button-variant(@color; @background; @border) {
```

The mixin does the following:

- Specifies the button font, background, and border colors (in other words, the three parameters that the mixin accepts)
- Generates hover, focus, active, and disabled states for the button, adjusting font color, background color, and border

If you'd like to, you can see how Bootstrap uses this mixin in `bootstrap/buttons.less` under the comment `// Alternate buttons`. Here are the lines generating styles for the default and primary buttons:

```
// Alternate buttons
// --------------------------------------------------
.btn-default {
  .button-variant(@btn-default-color; @btn-default-bg; @btn-default-border);
}
.btn-primary {
  .button-variant(@btn-primary-color; @btn-primary-bg; @btn-primary-border);
}
```

 You will find the variables beginning with `@btn-default-` and `@btn-primary-` in `variables.less`.

Following this pattern, we can generate our custom feature button in four simple steps:

1. First, we'll set up a new set of button variables. In `_variables.less`, under `// Buttons`, make a copy of the three `@btn-primary-` variables, and customize them, replacing `-primary-` with `-feature-` and using `@brand-feature` as the background color:

    ```
    @btn-feature-color:        #fff;
    @btn-feature-bg:           @brand-feature;
    @btn-feature-border:       darken
       (@btn-feature-bg, 5%);
    ```

2. Next, we can make a file to keep our custom buttons. Create _buttons-custom.less and write a mixin based on the .btn-primary mixin from bootstrap/buttons.less as follows:

```
.btn-feature {
  .button-variant(@btn-feature-color; @btn-feature-bg; @btn-feature-border);
}
```

3. Save this file and add it to the import sequence in __main.less as follows:

```
@import "bootstrap/buttons.less";
@import "_buttons-custom.less"; // added
```

4. Now, in index.html, change the button class from btn-primary to btn-feature. While we're at it, we want to make the button large, so add the class btn-lg:

```
<a class="btn btn-feature btn-lg pull-right" href="#">
  Learn more
```

Save. Refresh the browser, and you should see the following result. The primary column to the left now has a larger font size and a large button with our brand-feature color.

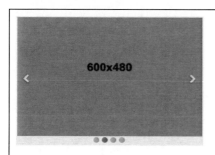

Meanwhile, the font size and button colors of the secondary (center) column are exactly what we want. What needs to happen next is this: we need to de-emphasize the tertiary column content so that it takes its appropriate place in the informational hierarchy.

Adjusting the tertiary column

Our task for the tertiary content is fairly straightforward. We have to reduce the font size and de-emphasize the buttons. This can be accomplished as follows:

1. First, we'll adjust the font-size. In `_variables.less`, adjust the `@font-size-small` variable:

   ```
   @font-size-small:          ceil(@font-size-base * 0.90);
   ```

2. Now we need only add these lines to `_page-contents.less`:

   ```
   .content-tertiary {
     font-size: @font-size-small;
   }
   ```

3. Save, compile, refresh, and you should see the font size reduce.

4. Next, in `index.html`, we need to edit our button classes. We'll change them from `btn-primary` to `btn-default`, and we'll reduce their size using the class `btn-xs`:

   ```
   <a class="btn btn-default btn-xs pull-right" href="#">Read more
   ...
   ```

   This will reduce the button size and turn the button background white.

5. Let's adjust the background to a light gray and adjust the font color and border as well. In `_variables.less`, adjust the values for the three `@btn-default-` variables as follows:

   ```
   @btn-default-color:        @gray;
   @btn-default-bg:           @gray-lightest;
   @btn-default-border:       darken
     (@btn-default-bg, 5%);
   ```

Save the changes, compile the file, and refresh your browser.

We now have a clear visual hierarchy, from the primary content (on the left), to the secondary (center) and tertiary (right).

Now, take a moment to notice that our adjustments work reasonably well in the narrow single-column layout as well:

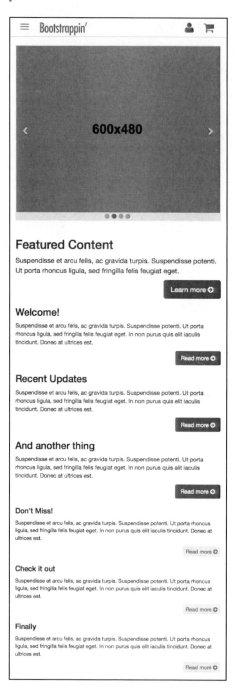

In narrow viewports, our three columns stretch out vertically, one after the other, with primary content first, followed by secondary and tertiary.

All that remains is some fine-tuning to make our content even more user friendly across devices and viewports.

Fine touches for multiple viewports

It's always good to give our content — and our viewers' eyes — some room to breathe. Visual indicators of section boundaries are good as well. Let's fold these in:

1. First, we'll add padding above and below our content. Add a bit of top padding to the `main` element itself. This padding will serve us well in all viewports, so we won't need a media query.

   ```
   main {
     padding-top: 20px;
     padding-bottom: 40px;
   }
   ```

2. Next, we need to set our columns to clear floated items above them when in single-column layout on narrow devices. Otherwise, the secondary and tertiary columns will overlap the button immediately above them. We'll write this within the appropriate media query to limit it to narrow viewports only:

   ```
   // Make columns clear floats in narrow viewport single-
     column layout
   @media (max-width: @screen-sm-min) {
     [class*="col-"] {
       clear: both;
     }
   }
   ```

That's it. Our main content layout is ready. Now for the complex footer area.

Laying out a complex footer

In the following steps, we'll create a complex footer built to manage multiple goals, including these: three lists of links to key sections of our website, a bit of **About Us** text, social icons, and our logo.

Setting up the markup

We will start by creating the footer markup. We want this footer to be as functional and useful for the user as possible. We'll build the markup as follows:

1. Find the file `footer-content.html` in the project folder `04_Code_BEGIN`. Open it in your editor, and copy the entire content to the clipboard.

2. Now, back in `index.html`, find the place where we want to paste this content. It's within `footer role="contentinfo"`, just after `div class="container"` and before `ul class="social"`. (I've placed a comment there to help you find the spot.)

3. Before pasting the content, let's prepare to utilize the Bootstrap grid system. To do this, we'll wrap the area within `div class="row"`, as follows:

```
<footer role="contentinfo">
  <div class="container">
    <div class="row">
      <!-- INSERT ADDITIONAL FOOTER CONTENT HERE -->
    </div><!-- /.row -->
    <ul class="social">
```

4. Now, paste the new content in place.

5. Next, we'll wrap each of the three lists of links along with their headings within `div` of class `col-md-2`. This way, each list will take one-sixth of the available width in medium and larger viewports. Together, these three lists will take half the available viewport width.

```
<div class="col-md-2">
  <h3>Categories</h3>
```

6. Now to complete our row, wrap the **About Us** heading and its paragraph in `div` of class `col-md-6` so that it takes up the remaining half of the available width:

```
<div class="about col-md-6">
  <h3>About Us</h3>
```

 Be sure to add the necessary closing tags for each new `div` element.

7. Save, refresh, and check your results.

In a viewport of 980px and larger, our columns should organize themselves as follows:

Categories	Styles	Other	About Us
• Shoes • Clothing • Accessories • Men • Women • Kids • Pets	• Athletic • Casual • Dress • Everyday • Other Days • Alternative • Otherwise	• Link • Another link • Link again • Try this • Don't you dare • Oh go ahead	Lorem ipsum dolor sit amet, consectetur adipiscing elit. Suspendisse euismod congue bibendum. Aliquam erat volutpat. Phasellus eget justo lacus. Vivamus pharetra ullamcorper massa, nec ultricies metus gravida egestas. Duis congue viverra arcu, ac aliquet turpis rutrum a. Donec semper vestibulum dapibus. Integer et sollicitudin metus. Vivamus at nisi turpis. Phasellus vel tellus id felis cursus hendrerit. Learn more ⊙

This is the layout we want in medium and larger viewports. Extra-small screen sizes are served just fine by the single-column layout. However, for tablet-width screen sizes that fall within the range of 768 to 980 pixels, our layout can benefit from some adjustments. Let's address that.

Adjusting for tablet-width viewports

Test the layout in a viewport that falls between 768 and 980 pixels. Bootstrap refers to this as the small breakpoint, with the `@screen-sm` variable and `col-sm-` grid classes. At this width, the single-column layout leaves unnecessary white space. Here is what you'll see:

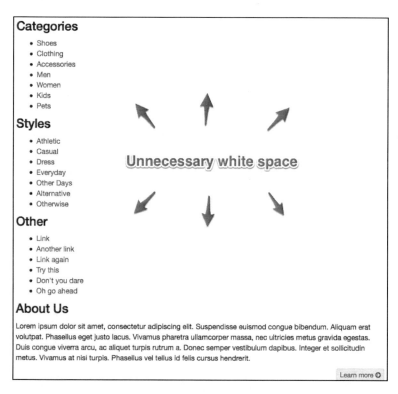

We can improve this layout by allowing our three lists of links to float next to each other. Using the Bootstrap `col-sm-` column classes, let's set the three lists of links to be one-third width, or `col-sm-4`, and the **About Us** column to be full width, or `col-sm-12`.

```
<div class="col-sm-4 col-md-2">
...
<div class="col-sm-4 col-md-2">
...
<div class="col-sm-4 col-md-2">
...
<div class="about col-sm-12 col-md-6">
```

Save this and try it out in the small viewport range. You will see the following result:

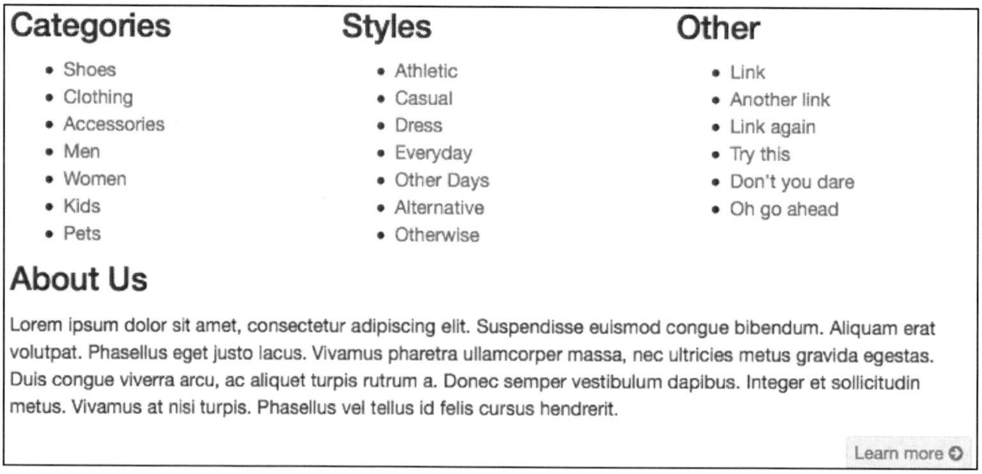

Much improved! But we're not quite finished. Try clicking on the links in the upper three columns. Chances are that you won't be able to. Inspect the element and you'll find that the fourth `div` element contains the code for the **About Us** column. This code does not clear the floated columns above it. Though the **About Us** heading and its paragraph will appear below the three floating columns, the `div` element itself will overlap them.

Adding a targeted responsive clearfix

In a standard Bootstrap layout situation, we would use a `div` element with the `row` class to clear the floating columns above. Here, we need a different solution, as we want this block of content to clear floats only within this specific breakpoint.

To accomplish this, we could write custom styles in our LESS files. But we can also use a Bootstrap responsive utility class to provide a targeted `clearfix` directly in the markup. Since we've already specified grid classes in our markup, let's use the second option in this context.

You can find the approach we'll use mentioned in Bootstrap's documentation at `http://getbootstrap.com/css/#grid-responsive-resets`. Following that method, we'll create a `div` element with the class `clearfix`, and add a Bootstrap responsive utility class to make it visible only on small screens. We'll place this new div element immediately prior to the **About Us** column:

```
<div class="clearfix visible-sm"></div>
<div class="about col-sm-12 col-md-6">
```

The `clearfix` class will force this element to clear the floats above it. The `visible-sm` class will allow this `div` to display only within our targeted breakpoint. At other breakpoints, it will be as if this `div` does not exist.

Save this, refresh your browser, and you should find that the **About Us** column now clears the floats above it and that the links are clickable.

Task complete. Now for a few finishing touches.

Refining the details

We have a few last touches we want to implement as we finish our footer. These include the following:

- Refining the presentation of our three lists of links
- Adjusting margins and padding
- Reversing the color scheme to match our navbar colors

To accomplish these refinements, we'll write some custom styles. Let's tackle this in cascading fashion, starting with general rules for the footer and moving to the specific rules:

1. Open `_footer.less`, the file for custom footer styles, in your editor.

   Here you'll find some initial rules that I've carried over with slight modifications from *Chapter 2, Bootstrappin' Your Portfolio*. These include some initial padding for the footer as well as styles for the social icons and the footer version of the logo.

2. Now to add the refinements we need for our new complex footer. Let's start by reducing the footer font size and inverting the color scheme to correspond with the inverted navbar—a blue background with light text. I'll begin with those colors and then darken them slightly. To do this, I'll make use of appropriate variables from _variables.less, including @font-size-small, @navbar-inverse-bg, and @navbar-inverse-color:

```
footer[role="contentinfo"] {
  padding-top: 24px;
  padding-bottom: 24px;
  font-size: @font-size-small;
  background-color: darken(@navbar-inverse-bg, 18%);
  color: darken(@navbar-inverse-color, 18%);
```

 In this and all that follows, we need to nest our new rules within footer[role="contentinfo"].

3. Next, we need to adjust our links and buttons to fit the new color scheme. Still nesting rules within footer[role="contentinfo"], I've done this as follows:

```
a {
  color: @navbar-inverse-color;
  &:focus,
  &:hover,
  &:active {
    color: @navbar-inverse-link-hover-color;
  }
}
.btn-default {
  color: darken(@navbar-inverse-bg, 18%) !important;
}
```

4. Now to address the four h3 headings. I'll adjust font size, trim the bottom margin, and convert the text to uppercase:

```
h3 {
  font-size: 120%;
  margin-bottom: 4px;
  text-transform: uppercase;
}
```

5. Having done this, we can next remove bullets from our list of links, and adjust their padding and margin.

```
ul {
  list-style: none;
  padding: 0;
  margin: 0;
}
```

 For the purposes of this exercise, I've applied these rules to all unordered lists within the site footer. Depending on the needs of your footer, you may want to use a special class for these lists of links, such as, footer-nav.

6. Lastly, let's adjust our social icons. We'll add a bit of top padding and then adjust their colors to work better with the new color scheme. Since these are Font Awesome icons, we can do this simply by adjusting the color and background-color values, as follows:

```
ul.social {
  ...
  padding: 24px 0 0;
  ...
  > li {
    ...
    > a {
      ...
      background-color: darken(@navbar-inverse-bg, 27%);
      color: darken(@navbar-inverse-color, 18%);
      ...
      &:hover {
        ...
        background-color: darken(@navbar-inverse-bg, 32%);
        color: @navbar-inverse-link-hover-color;
      }
    }
  }
}
```

That's it. Save, compile, refresh, and enjoy! Here is our result in medium and wide viewports:

And here is the result for small viewports:

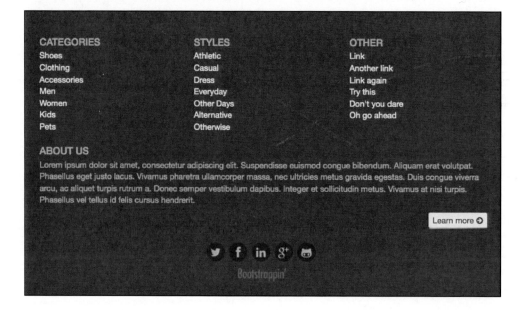

And this is for extra-small viewports:

Not bad! We have built a footer capable of managing a complex array of content across the full spectrum of extra-small, small, medium, and large viewports.

Summary

This project has enabled us to beef up our Bootstrappin' skills in a number of ways. We have covered the following:

- Styling a complex responsive navbar, so that it appears below the logo and banner area in medium and large viewports and yet collapses into a mobile-friendly navbar on smaller screens
- Building a custom responsive utility navbar, with text and icons that adapt creatively to suit the needs of larger and smaller screens
- Designing a responsive layout for the main content of our page, providing an appropriate visual hierarchy for three tiers of information
- Building a footer that effectively manages multiple blocks of links and text across viewports
- Enhancing our footer with a modified version of the inverted color scheme we used for the navbar

Congratulations! In the next chapter, we'll build on these skills by designing a products page suitable for an e-commerce section for this website.

5
Bootstrappin' E-commerce

Having built our business home page, it's time to design our online store.

We'll build on the design from the previous chapter, adding a new page with the following elements:

- A grid of product thumbnails, titles, and descriptions
- A left-hand sidebar with options to filter our products by category, brand, and so on
- Breadcrumbs and pagination to ease navigation through our inventory

Take a few moments to visit websites like Zappos (http://www.zappos.com) and Amazon (http://www.amazon.com). Search or browse for products and you will see product grids with features similar to what we will be creating in this chapter.

When complete, we want our products page to look like the following screenshot on small, medium, and large screens:

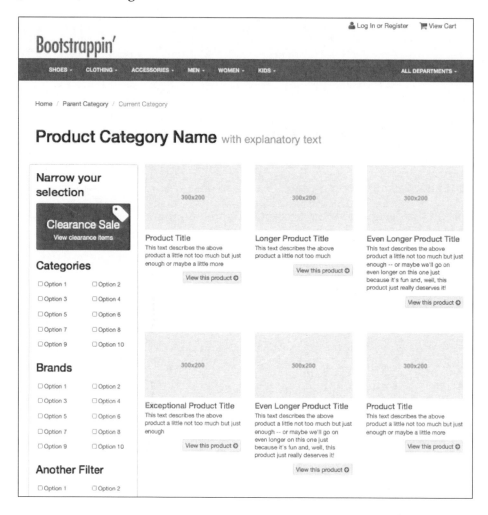

On extra-small screens, we want our products page to adjust to the following layout:

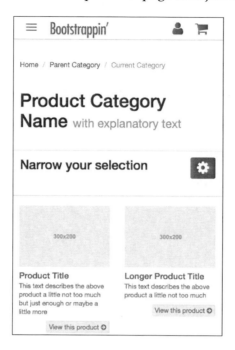

Bootstrap gives us a big head start in accomplishing this design—after which we can use the power of LESS to refine things to completion.

Surveying the markup for our products page

You'll find this chapter's files prepared and ready in the folder 05_Code_BEGIN. This project builds directly on the completed design from *Chapter 4, Bootstrappin' Business*. If anything in these files seems strange, you may want to review *Chapter 4, Bootstrappin' Business*, before proceeding.

> If you've not already downloaded the exercise files, you can find them at http://packtpub.com/support.

For this chapter, there is one new file in the main folder, `products.html`.

Open `products.html` in your editor to view the markup. Let's survey its contents.

The head, header, and navbar elements are consistent with what we've already seen in *Chapter 4, Bootstrappin' Business*. Inside the `main role="main"` element is where we'll find what's new. Here, you'll find the following elements in the same order as they appear:

- Breadcrumb links marked up as an unordered list
- A page title within an `h1` heading
- A series of options for filtering products
- Nine products with thumbnails, titles, descriptions, and a button
- An unordered list of pagination links just below the products and before the site footer

If you view the file in your browser, you'll see that much remains to be done. Breadcrumbs do not yet look like breadcrumbs, the filtering options look like a long series of bulleted lists, the layout of our product items is uneven (and in places broken), and so on.

Don't let these current imperfections worry you. These are the things that we'll be addressing in the following steps. Here is what's coming:

- We will apply Bootstrap's built-in styles to the breadcrumbs, page title, and pagination, and then customize them further

- We will improve the layout of the nine product items, innovating the Bootstrap grid system to maintain a visually well-organized grid across breakpoints

- We will style the filtering options by enhancing the layout and then using the Font Awesome icons to provide checkboxes

Now that we have a plan, let's get started!

Styling the breadcrumbs, page title, and pagination

In the following steps, we'll apply Bootstrap styles to our breadcrumbs, page title, and pagination, and then customize them to fit our design:

1. Open `products.html` in your editor.

2. Find the unordered list just above the `h1` page title, add the class `"breadcrumb"` to the `ul` tag, and then add the class `"active"` to the last list item, as follows:

```
<ul class="breadcrumb">
  <li><a href="#">Home</a></li>
  <li><a href="#">Parent Category</a></li>
  <li class="active">Current Category</li>
</ul>
```

These classes correspond with Bootstrap breadcrumb styles, which you will find documented at `http://getbootstrap.com/components/#breadcrumbs`.

Save and refresh your browser. You should see the result as shown in the following screenshot:

Home / Parent Category / Current Category

3. To customize the breadcrumbs for this design, let's remove the light gray background and the extra padding. For such a quick adjustment, we'll work directly in `breadcrumbs.less` in the `bootstrap` folder, leaving a trail by commenting out the unneeded lines.

Let's set the `padding` to `0` and remove the `background-color` entirely, commenting out the former values so that we can clearly see what we've done:

```
.breadcrumb {
  padding: 0; // 8px 15px; // edited
  margin-bottom: @line-height-computed;
  list-style: none;
  // background-color: @breadcrumb-bg; // edited
```

4. Now for the page title. Bootstrap's page title works by nesting the top-level page heading within a `div` tag of the `page-header` class. You can see the documentation at `http://getbootstrap.com/components/#page-header`.

    Let's adjust our markup accordingly. Let's also add some text within a `small` tag to take advantage of the Bootstrap style for adding the explanatory notes to our headings:

```
<div class="page-header">
  <h1>Product Category Name <small>with explanatory
    text</small></h1>
</div>
```

    That will produce the following result:

> **Product Category Name** <small>with explanatory text</small>

5. Let's keep the margin and padding that comes with the page header, but remove the bottom border. Open the `type.less` file placed in the `bootstrap` folder. Search for `.page-header` and comment out the `border-bottom` rule:

```
.page-header {

  // border-bottom: 1px solid @page-header-border-color;
}
```

    Save, refresh, and you should see a result that is cleaner — with ample white space that fits our overall design — as shown in the following screenshot:

> Home / Parent Category / Current Category
>
> **Product Category Name** <small>with explanatory text</small>

6. Finally, the pagination. Our markup for this is found just a few lines above the closing main tag (`</main>`). Above that closing tag, you'll see commented closing div tags for the `.container`, `.row`, and `.products-grid`:

```
      </div><!-- /.products-grid -->
    </div><!-- /.row -->
  </div><!-- /.container -->
</main>
```

Bootstrap's documentation for pagination styles is found at `http://getbootstrap.com/components/#pagination`.

To apply these styles here, we only need to add `class="pagination"` to the ul tag that you will find a few lines above the closing `.products-grid` tag:

```
<ul class="pagination">
  <li><a href="#"><span class="fa fa-chevron-left"></span>
    Prev</a></li>
  <li><a href="#">1</a></li>
  <li><a href="#">2</a></li>
  <li><a href="#">3</a></li>
  <li><a href="#">4</a></li>
  <li><a href="#">Next <span class="fa fa-chevron-
    right"></span></a></li>
</ul>
```

 For the Next and Prev items, I've already provided the span tags for the Font Awesome icons `fa-chevron-left` and `-right`.

This gives us the result as shown in the following screenshot:

7. Let's center align the pagination below our grid. First, wrap it in a parent div tag. We'll place the row class on this to ensure it clears the content above it, and then we'll add an appropriately named custom class `pagination-wrap`:

```
<div class="row pagination-wrap">
  <ul class="pagination">
    <li> ...
  </ul>
</div>
```

8. Now, we need some custom styling to center align this component within its space. In *Chapter 4, Bootstrappin' Business*, we used the custom LESS file `_page-contents.less` to write our custom styles. Here, let's create a more specific file to manage the special features for our products grid. Create a new file called `_products-grid.less`, save it in the `less` folder alongside our other custom LESS files, and add the following lines to it:

```less
.pagination-wrap {
    text-align: center;
}
```

Save the file.

9. Now we'll add the new file to our LESS import sequence. Open the `_main.less` file inside the `less` folder, and add the import line under the comment `// Other custom files`, as shown here:

```less
@import "_products-grid.less"; // added
```

Save the file and compile to CSS.

Refresh your browser. You should now see our pagination snap to the center.

Adjusting the products grid

Let's make our products grid look as it should. If you inspect the markup for our product items, you'll see that each has been given a class of `col-sm-4`:

```html
<div class="product-item col-sm-4">
```

While this constrains the width of each of our product items, it has failed to produce an effective grid.

The primary problem here is that our items have varying heights. Thus, when trying to float left, as Bootstrap grid components do, these items bump into one another. This results in a broken, uneven layout as shown in the following screenshot:

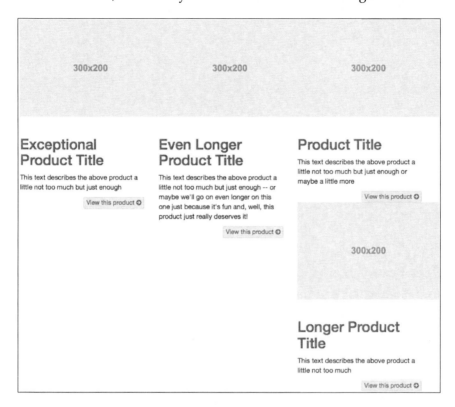

Currently, in a medium and large viewport, product items 4 to 7 refuse to float neatly due to their uneven heights.

Let's adjust the styles of our grid items to enhance their visual presentation. Having done that, we can fix this layout problem.

1. As we'll be writing custom styles, have _products-grid.less open in your editor.

2. Let's write styles to adjust image width, font size, padding, and margins as shown in the following lines of code:

```
.product-item {
  padding-bottom: 32px;
  img {
    width: 100%;
  }
}
```

```less
h2 {
  font-size: @font-size-large;
  line-height: 1.2;
  padding: 0 !important;
  margin-top: 6px;
  margin-bottom: 2px;
  }
p {
  font-size: @font-size-small;
  line-height: 1.3;
  color: @gray;
  }
}
```

3. These styles will accomplish the following:
   - Add bottom padding to each product item
   - Constrain the thumbnail image to the width of the product item
   - Reduce the h2 heading font size to the size of our @font-size-large
   - Reduce the p font size to our @font-size-small value
   - Reduce h2 padding by adding !important to override any conflicting rules that we've written to apply in the standard pages
   - Set the p font color to @gray

Save these new styles, compile to CSS, and refresh your browser. Though the layout will still be broken in places, you should see significant improvement in the styling of the product items as shown in the following screenshot:

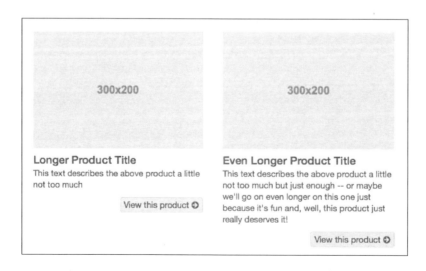

4. Now, let's fix our layout problem. We'll do this simply by finding the maximum height that we need to manage the content of our test items. We are going to assume that we are working in a context where there are established guidelines for the images and text, so all product items will have standard thumbnail sizes and use no more text than the wordiest of the examples used here. If that is the case, then we can set a height value either in pixels or perhaps in more dynamic units, such as em or ex. For the purpose of this exercise, let's use the value of 360px. While we're at it, let's hide content that overflows this value in order to avoid the potential problem of content messily overlapping the boundaries between items. Because these rules are focused on layout, I'll write them as a separate set of rules, albeit still in _products-grid.less, as follows:

```
.product-item {
    height: 360px;
    overflow: hidden;
}
```

Save the file, compile to CSS, and refresh your browser. You should see our layout problems go away! The result is shown in the following screenshot:

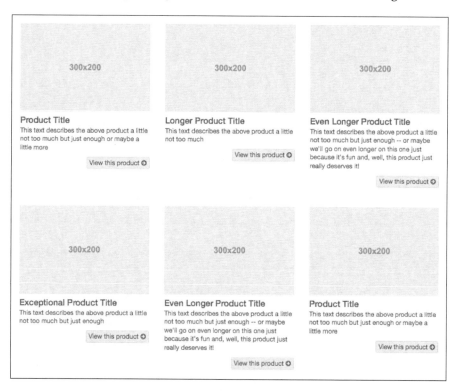

5. From this point, we can simply use responsive Bootstrap column classes in our markup to adjust as necessary across viewport widths. In this case, we want our grid to reduce to two products per row for small and extra-small screens, while medium and large viewports will have three items per row. To accomplish this, we need to find and replace the classes in each of our product items so that they are as follows:

```
<div class="product-item col-xs-6 col-md-4">
```

These classes will set each product item to half width within extra-small and small viewports, and then transition to one-third width for medium and large viewports.

Save the file and refresh your browser. You should now be able to drag to make your window width smaller or larger and watch the adjustment happen dynamically.

Product items will now be laid out in two columns on small and extra-small viewports.

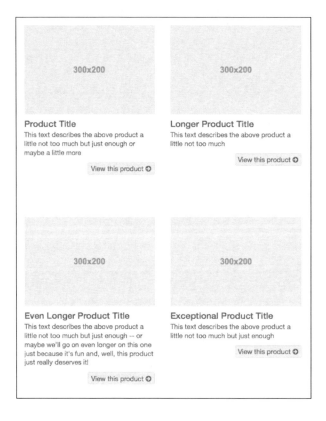

Then, our grid will transition to a three-column layout in medium and large viewports.

It's a beautiful thing to behold.

Next, we'll style the filtering options sidebar.

Styling the options sidebar

Now, let's style our filtering options. These appear just before the markup for our product items. In small, medium, and large viewports, they appear as a left-hand sidebar.

At the moment, they appear like the following screenshot:

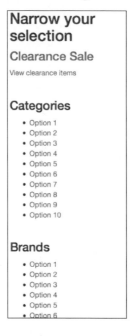

For our final design, we want to transform the **Clearance Sale** link into an attractive extra-large button and arrange the filtering options into two columns with checkboxes rather than bullets, as shown in the following screenshot:

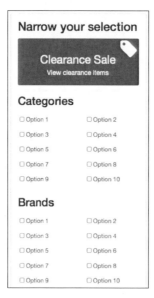

Let's begin by setting up some basic styles to lay a basic groundwork.

Setting up basic styles

We'll start by adjusting fonts, colors, margins, and padding.

Let's add these rules to `_products-grid.less`:

```
.grid-options {
  .panel;
  .panel-default;
  padding-top: 12px;
  padding-bottom: 24px;
  > h2 {
    margin-top: 0;
    font-size: 1.5 * (@font-size-large);
    line-height: 1.2;
    color: @gray-dark;
  }
}
```

The preceding code does the following:

- Adds Bootstrap default panel styles to our sidebar (see the relevant Bootstrap documentation at `http://getbootstrap.com/components/#panels`)
- Adds top and bottom padding to the sidebar so that our new background extends past the sidebar content
- Adjusts font size, line-height, and color for the h2 heading

Next, we will style the **Clearance Sale** link.

Styling the Clearance Sale link

We want to transform our **Clearance Sale** link into an extra-large attractive button.

Let's adjust the markup to do the following:

- Turn the linked heading and paragraph into a button.
- Add the custom button `btn-feature` class, which we created in *Chapter 4, Bootstrappin' Business*, to give the button our special featured color — red.
- Add a Font Awesome icon for a sale tag. We'll make it three times the normal size by using Font Awesome's built-in `icon-3x` class.

 For more information about Font Awesome's special sizing classes, see the documentation at `http://fontawesome.io/examples/#larger`.

The resulting markup is as follows:

```
<a class="btn btn-feature choose-clearance" href="#">
  <span class="icon fa fa-tag fa-3x"></span>
  <h3>Clearance Sale</h3>
  <p>View clearance items</p>
</a>
```

This immediately gives us a good start towards our desired result as shown in the following screenshot:

Now to polish it up, perform the following steps:

1. Display the **Clearance Sale** button as a block-level element and center it using the `.center-block()` Bootstrap mixin.

2. Force its width to fill 92.5 percent of its containing column.

3. Add top and bottom padding.

4. Override Bootstrap's `white-space: nowrap` rule for buttons, so that our text can wrap as it should (See Bootstrap's `white-space` rule in `less/bootstrap/buttons.less`. You can learn more about the `white-space` property at `http://css-tricks.com/almanac/properties/w/whitespace/`).

5. Position it relative so that we can apply absolute positioning to the tag icon.

6. Adjust font, color, and margins on our heading and paragraph.

7. Position the tag icon at the top right.

We can accomplish these goals by adding the following style rules:

```
.choose-clearance {
  .center-block();
   width: 92.5%;
  padding-top: 20px;
  padding-bottom: 12px;
  white-space: normal;
  position: relative;
  h3 {
```

```
        font-weight: normal;
        color: #fff;
        padding-top: 4px;
        margin: 6px;
    }
  p {
        margin: 6px 20px;
        line-height: 1.2;
    }
    .icon {
        position: absolute;
        top: 0;
        right: 2px;
    }
    }
    }
```

This gives us a pleasing result as is evident from the following screenshot:

As a bonus, these styles work well across viewport sizes. Take a few moments to test it. Then of course, as always, feel free to take what we've begun and beautify it further.

Meanwhile, let's move down to the options for filtering our products.

Styling the options list

In this section, we will transform our lists of product filtering options.

If you take a moment to examine the markup of product filtering options in a store such as Amazon (http://www.amazon.com) or Zappos (http://www.zappos.com), you'll find that they are composed lists of links that have been specially styled to appear like checkboxes. We will style our links to look like checkboxes, which will appear as checked once selected, and we'll adjust them to work nicely across devices, such as tablet and phone devices.

On e-commerce websites such as Amazon and Zappos.com, the filter options are connected to a content management system, which dynamically updates the grid of shown products in response to the options selected. Bootstrap is a frontend design framework, and not a content management system. Thus, we will not be dynamically filtering our products as a part of this project. Instead, we will prepare a design that is ready to be used in the context of a complete content management system.

We'll start with the `h3` headings for the lists, adjusting their size, line-height, margin, and color:

```
.grid-options {
  > h3 {
    font-size: @font-size-large;
    line-height: 1.2;
    margin-top: 12px;
    color: @gray-dark;
  }
}
```

We need to use the >h3 child selector since we don't want these rules to apply to other h3 tags, especially the one within our **Clearance Sale** button.

Now, let's turn our attention to the unordered lists. These have a special class of `options-list`, which we'll use as our selector to ensure we're targeting only these special lists.

First, let's remove bullets and padding:

```
.grid-options {
  ..
  .options-list {
    list-style-type: none;
    padding-left: 0;
  }
}
```

Now we'll style the links. Shortly, we'll also style the list items, so we'll include them in the sequence of nested selectors.

```
...
  li {
      a {
          .btn;
```

```
       .btn-sm;
       padding-left: 0;
       padding-right: 0;
       color: @gray;
   }
  &:hover,
 &:focus,
 &:active,
 .active & {
color: @link-color;
 }
}
```

The rules we just set accomplish the following:

- We'll use the power of LESS to pull in the fundamental button styles associated with the `.btn` class that includes displaying the `inline-block` link and the addition of padding:
  - Since we added no other button class, there is no background color
  - What we gain from these basic button styles is a convenient way to make our links user-friendly click targets—including fingers on touch devices
- We then pull in the styles associated with the `.btn-sm` class to reduce padding and for the font-size to be a bit smaller than the standard button (for a refresher on Bootstrap button classes, go to `http://getbootstrap.com/css/#buttons`)
- We then remove unneeded left and right padding
- We change the color of our link text to `@gray`
- Finally, we set the color of hovered, focused, and active links to our `@link-color` value

You may want to save, compile, and test the results. The following screenshot depicts the result we get:

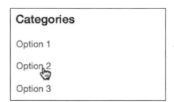

Our option links have gained improved padding and font size and taken our desired colors.

 You may be wondering why I've chosen to pull in button styles by using the `.btn` and `.btn-sm` classes in our LESS files rather than adding the classes directly in the markup. We could do the latter, but given the number of option links, I think you will agree that it is far more efficient to apply the styles via CSS as we've done. In the section that follows, I will continue this pattern and extend it by bringing in Font Awesome icons via LESS rather than by adding markup.

Now we'll add checkboxes to our option links.

Adding Font Awesome checkboxes to our option links

In this section, we'll use Font Awesome icons to add an empty checkbox to the left of each option link. Rather than adding icons in the markup, we will do it here via LESS as it will be far more efficient. Then we'll push a step further, adding styles to pull in an alternate Font Awesome icon—for a checked checkbox — to the hovered, focused, and active option links.

Adding icons via LESS requires drawing Font Awesome styles from three files. First, we will take these fundamental styles from the `core.less` file in the `font-awesome` folder. In this file, you'll find the following key styles:

```
.@{fa-css-prefix} {
  display: inline-block;
  font-family: FontAwesome;
  font-style: normal;
  font-weight: normal;
  line-height: 1;
  -webkit-font-smoothing: antialiased;
  -moz-osx-font-smoothing: grayscale;
}
```

These styles establish the fundamental rules for all Font Awesome icons, including the Font Awesome icon for the font family and then refine the details of its presentation.

For our present purposes, we do not need the selector or the braces but only the rules. We will take these and apply them to our links. Primarily, we'll use the `:before` pseudo-element as it ensures the best results.

 For more information about the CSS2.1 `:before` pseudo-element, go to `http://coding.smashingmagazine.com/2011/07/13/learning-to-use-the-before-and-after-pseudo-elements-in-css/`.

Copy the rules (but not the selector) from `core.less`. Then paste these rules in the `_products-grid.less` file, nested as follows:

```
.grid-options {
    ...
    li {
        ...
        a {
            ...
            &:before {
                // from font-awesome/core.less
                display: inline-block;
                font-family: FontAwesome;
                font-style: normal;
                font-weight: normal;
                line-height: 1;
                -webkit-font-smoothing: antialiased;
                -moz-osx-font-smoothing: grayscale;
```

These rules establish the fundamentals. Next, we need to specify which Font Awesome icon to use. Browsing the options at `http://fontawesome.io/icons/`, we find the following open checkbox icon:

The LESS rules for this icon are found in the `icons.less` file inside the font-awesome folder. By opening that file and searching for the string `}-square-o` (including the closing curly brace before `-square-o` to narrow the results), we can find the following relevant line:

```
.@{fa-css-prefix}-square-o:before { content: @fa-var-square-o; }
```

From the previous line, we need only `content: @fa-var-square-o`, which we need to copy and paste in the `_products-grid.less` file directly after the preceding rules are applied to our `a:before` selector:

```
a {
    ...
    &:before {
        ...
        content: @fa-var-square-o;
```

Finally, we want to grab Font Awesome styles to give our icons a fixed width and to avoid any shifting when the icon changes to the checked version. These styles are found in the `fixed-width.less` file inside the `font-awesome` folder. Copy and paste just these two lines while also applying them to our `&:before` selector:

```
width: (18em / 14);
text-align: center;
```

After adding these rules, compile them to CSS and refresh your browser. You should see the checkboxes appear as shown in the following screenshot:

Now, following the same approach, we'll add the following selectors and rules to apply the checked version of the Font Awesome icon to the hovered, focused, and active states of our links:

```
li {
    ...
    a {
        &:before {
            ...
            content: @fa-var-square-o;

        &:hover:before,
        &:focus:before,
        &:active:before,
        .active &:before {
            content: @fa-var-check-square-o;
        }
```

Save the file, compile to CSS, and refresh your browser. You'll find that the checked version of the square icon appears when you hover on one of the links as shown in the following screenshot:

 As a reminder, it is not currently possible to force one of these links to stay in the active state as we have no content management system in place. What we do have is a set of styles ready and waiting to go to work in the context of such a content management system.

That's it! We've successfully given our links the appearance of checkboxes to provide desired user feedback.

Next, let's make more efficient use of our space by floating our options side by side.

Using LESS mixins to arrange option links in columns

In the previous section, we've used custom LESS rules to accomplish steps that might have been accomplished by adding markup. Given the number of option links we need to manage, this has proven significantly more efficient. The same dynamic applies when we want to arrange our option links into columns.

We might accomplish our desired result by using Bootstrap row and column classes, adjusting our markup with the following pattern:

```
<ul class="options-list options-categories row">
    <li class="col-xs-6"><a href="#">Option 1</a></li>
    <li class="col-xs-6"><a href="#">Option 2</a></li>
    ...
```

Thanks to the power of Bootstrap's mixins, we can accomplish the same result with a few lines of LESS as shown in the following steps:

1. First, we'll apply the .make-row() mixin to the .options-list selector, as follows:

```
.options-list {
    .make-row();
    ...
```

This mixin applies the same styles to our options list that we would have gained by applying the `row` class in the markup. In this case, it's simply more efficient to do it here.

2. Next, we can use a **`.make-xs-col()`** mixin to apply column rules to our list items as follows:

```
li {
   .make-xs-column(6);
```

This will apply the same styles to our list items as would be applied if we had added the `col-xs-6` class to each of the relevant `li` tags.

3. After adding the preceding lines, save the file, compile to CSS, and refresh your browser. You should see the option links line up in two columns.

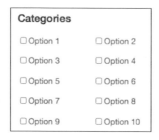

Not bad!

We will now make some adjustments for smaller viewports.

Adjusting the options list layout for tablets and phones

We need to constrain the width of our options panel so that it does not range too widely in tablet-width devices.

Right now, our **Clearance Sale** button stretches too wide, and our options list items spread too far apart on viewports between 480 pixels and 768 pixels wide. Thus, they can end up appearing like the following screenshot:

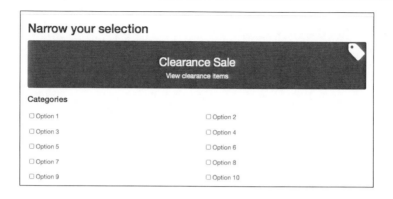

This can be easily fixed by setting a max-width property with a value of 480 pixels for the entire options panel:

```
.grid-options {
    ...
   max-width: 480px;
```

Now let's adjust our option list items so that they organize themselves in three columns in small viewports. Using LESS, we can nest a media query within the appropriate selector and add an adjusted .make-xs-column(4) mixin as shown in the following code snippet:

```
li {
    .make-xs-column(6);
    @media screen and (max-width: @screen-xs-max) {
    .make-xs-column(4);
    }
```

After making these adjustments, save the file, compile to CSS, and test in a narrow viewport. You should see the result as shown in the following screenshot:

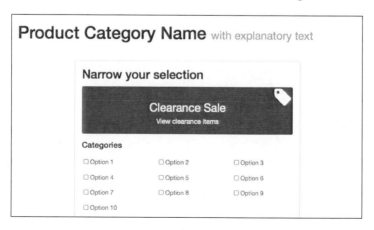

Now let's address the next problem facing our single-column layout: we need to hide our options away until they're needed.

Collapsing the options panel for phone users

At present, our options take up a considerable amount of vertical space. This creates a problem in narrow viewports. The single-column layout winds up pushing our grid of products far down the page.

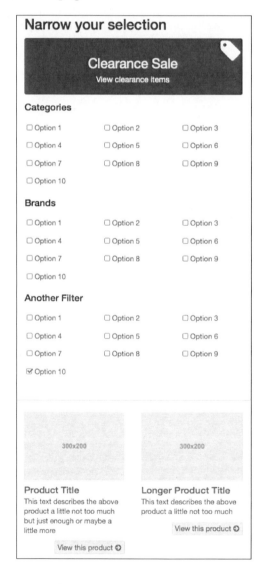

This is a great deal of vertical space for options that are not needed. The products themselves are priority items. We need to allow users of phones to find the products more quickly while still allowing them to access the filtering options when desired.

We'll use Bootstrap's collapse plugin for this. In the following steps, we'll apply the collapse plugin to the options panel, add a button to expand the panel when desired, and restrict the behavior to narrow viewports only:

1. Open your editor with `products.html`.

2. Add a new `div` tag to wrap our **Clearance Sale** button and three options lists. We need to give this new `div` a special class of collapse as well as a distinctive ID so that we can target it with our JavaScript plugin. For good measure, we'll give it a matching special class as well:

```
<div id="options-panel" class="options-panel collapse">
    <a class="btn btn-feature choose-clearance" href="#">
    ...
    <h3>Categories</h3>
    <ul class="options-list options-categories">
        <li><a href="#">Option 10</a></li>
        ...
    </ul>
</div><!-- /#options-panel.collapse -->
```

> Bootstrap's collapse JavaScript plugin is what powers the collapsible responsive navbar. It may also be put to other uses, such as the one shown in the Bootstrap's documentation at `http://getbootstrap.com/javascript/#collapse`.

3. Save the file and refresh it in your browser. You should see that the **Clearance Sale** button and options lists will now be hidden from view. All that remains of the options panel content will be the h2 heading **Narrow your selection** as shown in the following screenshot:

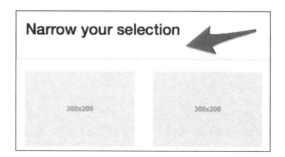

Now we need a toggle button to expand our filter options when clicked.

4. Within the still visible h2 heading that reads, **Narrow your selection**, add a button element with the following attribute structure:

```
<h2 class="clearfix">Narrow your selection
  <button type="button"
  class="options-panel-toggle btn btn-primary pull-right"
    data-toggle="collapse" data-target="#options-panel">
  <span class="icon fa fa-cog fa-2x"></span>
  </button>
</h2>
```

The following points explain what the preceding markup will do:

- The clearfix class will ensure that the h2 heading will contain the toggle button, which will float to the right (you'll find the clearfix class in the utilities.less file inside the bootstrap folder, the mixin of which it's made is in mixins.less in the bootstrap folder)

- The btn and btn-primary classes will style our new button element with the Bootstrap's btn styles, which includes our background color of @brand-primary

- The pull-right class will float the button to the right

- Within the button element, we've placed a Font Awesome cog icon using the fa-2x class to double its size

Save this and refresh to view the following result:

5. Now, we need to set rules to hide the toggle button and expand the options panel form medium to large screens. We can do this by adding the following lines to _products-grid.less:

```
// Responsive adjustments
@media (min-width: @screen-sm-min) {
    .options-panel {
        display: block;
    }
    .options-panel-toggle {
        display: none;
    }
}
```

6. This accomplishes the following goals:

  ° The media query will apply these rules only to small viewports and larger

  ° The first rule counteracts the `collapse` class, which hides its element by default

  ° The second rule hides the toggle button

Save and refresh, and you should see our desired results.

In narrow viewports, the options list is collapsed and the toggle button is visible:

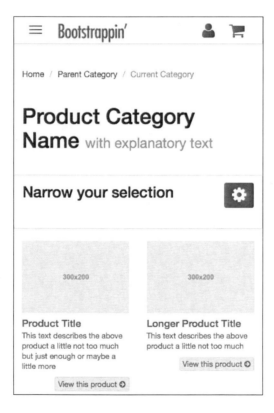

In small, medium, and large viewports, the toggle button is hidden, and the options list is visible:

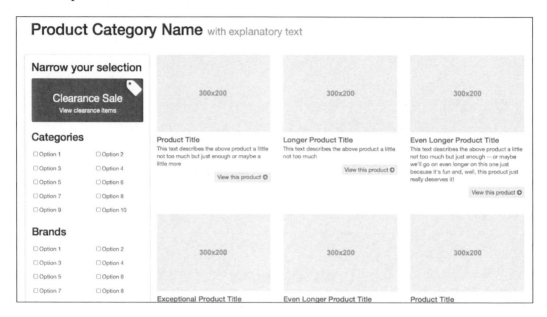

Congratulations! With this, we have accomplished our design.

Summary

In this chapter, we have done the following:

- Employed Bootstrap styles to quickly set up breadcrumbs, a page title, and pagination customized according to our needs

- Adjusted Bootstrap grid styles to create a visually pleasing grid of product items, all of the same height so as to ensure a regular grid

- Styled a complex **Clearance Sale** button with `@brand-feature` red background color

- Used the styles from the `btn` class to make our filter options more easily clickable, while customizing the styles to suit our needs

- Used Bootstrap column classes with responsive adjustments to arrange our options list items optimally for multiple viewport widths

- Used Font Awesome styles in the context of our own custom stylesheet in order to add checkboxes beside our filter options
- Set our options panel to collapse for viewers with narrow viewports, while remaining visible for small viewports and larger ones

Congratulations! We now have an attractive business website with a well-crafted e-commerce section.

Next, let's take our skills another step forward by creating a single page marketing website in the next chapter.

6
Bootstrappin' a One-page Marketing Website

We've developed some significant skills with Bootstrap. Now it's time to bring an extra touch of beauty and creativity to help our clients achieve their full online marketing potential. So, let's create a beautiful one-page upscale marketing site.

We'll cover the following things in this chapter:

- A large introductory carousel with a customized responsive welcome message
- A section for customer reviews with images and captions laid out in the masonry format
- A features list with large Font Awesome icons
- A signup section with custom-designed pricing tables
- A ScrollSpy navbar with animated scrolling behavior

Overview

We've been approached by a new prospective client. She is stricken by the beauty of one-pagers—websites that scroll vertically, providing a visually stimulating presentation of a product or message with a clear call to action at the end. She wants one of these.

This client is knowledgeable and discerning. She frequents `http://onepagelove.com` and has a list of her current favorites in hand. Her desired features include:

- A clean, modern aesthetic website.
- An introductory welcome message with a visually intriguing background image.

- An efficient presentation of the main features of her product, accentuated with visually appealing icons.

- Customer testimony presented in a visually stimulating way.

- An easy-to-understand overview of three basic packages that a customer can choose from. These need to be presented clearly in a way that makes it easy to choose the right fit and then sign up!

- Conversions! Everything should draw the user down the page, making it nearly impossible to avoid clicking on the sign up button at the end.

To protect the secrecy of her upcoming product launch, our client has chosen not to reveal the exact nature of her product or service to us. Rather, she has provided mockups of the design she would like us to create by using a dummy copy for placeholders.

The first section will open with an interesting full-width image, a large welcome message, and an invitation to scroll down the page to learn more, as shown in the following screenshot:

The second section will list six key features of the product, which are laid out in a three-column grid, and illustrate appropriate icons as shown in the following screenshot:

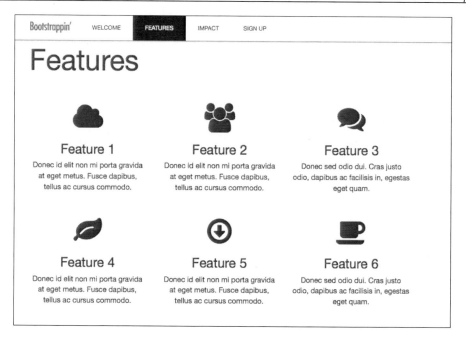

The third section will feature client testimonies with photos and quotations laid out in the masonry style:

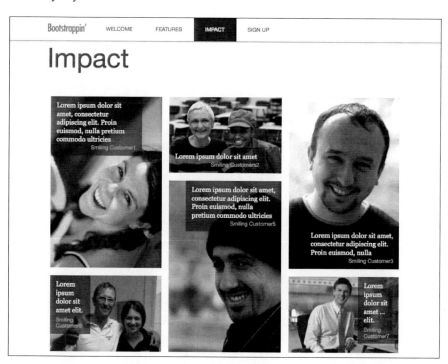

The fourth and final section will feature three available plans, each with a pricing table, and will have a visual emphasis on the center of the three tables, as shown in the following screenshot:

The savvy client that she is, she further demands that the design adapt beautifully to tablets and phones.

A great plan. No problem. Let's get to work.

Surveying the starter files

The files for this project are found in the `06_Code_Begin` exercise files. As in all previous projects, Bootstrap 3 LESS, JavaScript, and markup patterns provide the core of our code base, rounded out by the HTML5 Boilerplate and Font Awesome icon font.

The folder and file structure is very similar to what we've used in the previous projects in this book. Let me briefly recap some of the features of our LESS files:

- Default Bootstrap files are in the `/less/bootstrap/` folder.
- The LESS files of the Font Awesome icon font are found in `/less/font-awesome/`.

- Our custom LESS files are found directly inside the `less` folder and begin with an underscore, making it easy to spot them. Custom LESS files here include:
  - ◦ `__main.less`: This is the main file that imports all the others and is the file that you should compile to `css/main.css`
  - ◦ `_variables.less`: This is based on Bootstrap's variables with a few customizations
  - ◦ `_navbar.less`: This provides navbar customization
  - ◦ `_page-contents.less`: This provides styles for the content area of our pages
  - ◦ `_footer.less`: This provides styles for the footer area of our pages

You will have seen the preceding features in previous projects.

Here is what's distinctive about this set of files:

- I've applied a few custom LESS touches that are specific to this project:
  - ◦ `_variables.less`: I have adjusted a number of variables, especially for the navbar. I've sought to indicate these with comments.
  - ◦ `_navbar.less`: This constrains the size of the site logo image and lays it at the beginning of a visual aesthetic that fits our assignment.
- The `index.html` file has much of the markup we need already in place.
- Images are provided in the `img` folder. They've been scaled, cropped, and optimized for the Web and are already plugged into their appropriate places in the markup.

Before we begin, let's see how this currently appears in a web browser.

Viewing the page content

Open `index.html` in your browser. You'll see the following major components in place. Of course, at present, they will be displayed with default Bootstrap styles, awaiting the customization that needs to be done.

- A fixed top navbar
- A jumbotron with a big welcome message
- A features section with icons, headings, and text organized in three columns
- The **Impact** section with photos of six happy customers and placeholder content for their bits of positive testimony

- A **Sign up Now!** section with three tables laying out the **Basic Plan**, **Premium Plan**, and **Pro Plan** packages, with a **Sign up Now!** button under each
- A footer logo
- Photo credits (images are attribution licensed)

To view the markup, open `index.html` in your editor. We will get very familiar with the markup in the steps that follow!

Adjusting the navbar

This design calls for a fixed top navbar with a significant color shift for hovered and active links. I've already applied some of these styles by setting appropriate variables. Let me point those out, and then we'll move on to make some necessary adjustments to the markup.

The `less/_variables.less` file is based on Bootstrap's `variables.less` file. I've customized the shades of gray as per previous projects. You'll see these in the topmost section of the file.

I've further adjusted the following navbar variables, adjusting its height, margin, colors, and hover colors specifically for this design:

```
// Basics of a navbar
@navbar-height:                    56px;
@navbar-margin-bottom:             0;
...
// Navbar links
@navbar-default-link-color:        @navbar-default-color;
@navbar-default-link-hover-color:  #fff;
@navbar-default-link-hover-bg:     @gray;
@navbar-default-link-active-color: #fff;
@navbar-default-link-active-bg:    @gray-dark;
```

In addition, I've adjusted the variables for the navbar toggle:

```
// Navbar toggle
@navbar-default-toggle-hover-bg:      transparent;
@navbar-default-toggle-icon-bar-bg:   @gray-lighter;
@navbar-default-toggle-border-color:  transparent;
```

Finally, I've eliminated rounded corners from the navbar toggle as well as from any other elements in this design. This was easily accomplished by adjusting the three `@border-radius-` variables:

```
@border-radius-base:          0; // was 4px
@border-radius-large:         0; // was 6px
@border-radius-small:         0; // was 3px
```

Along with the custom variables, I've made a few adjustments to `_navbar.less`. I've adjusted the padding around `.navbar-brand` to allow the necessary space for our logo image:

 I've commented out the original line and then added a comment after the new line.

```
.navbar-brand {
  float: left;
  // padding: @navbar-padding-vertical @navbar-padding-horizontal;
  padding: 12px 30px 0 15px; // to allow for logo image
```

I've also customized the list items in the expanded navbar, adding left and right padding and transforming the text to uppercase:

```
// Uncollapse the nav
  @media (min-width: @grid-float-breakpoint) {
  ...
    > li {
      float: left;
      > a {
        padding-top: ((@navbar-height - @line-height-computed) / 2);
        padding-bottom: ((@navbar-height - @line-height-computed)
          / 2);
        padding-left: 24px; // added
        padding-right: 24px; // added
        text-transform: uppercase; // added
      }
    }
```

When combined, the adjusted variables and navbar customizations yield these visual results:

Let's proceed on to the jumbotron with its big welcome message.

Customizing the jumbotron

In this section, we'll customize the jumbotron to display our client's big welcome message with stylistic touches inline with her mockup. This will include adding a large background image, enlarging the welcome message text, and then adjusting its presentation for multiple viewports.

In `index.html`, find the following markup:

```
<!-- INTRO SECTION -->
<section id="welcome" class="jumbotron">
  <div class="container">
    <h1><strong>Big</strong> Welcome Message</h1>
    <p>Ingenious marketing copy. And some <em>more</em> ingenious
      marketing copy.<a href="#features" class="btn btn-lg btn-
      primary pull-right">Learn more <span class="icon fa fa-
      arrow-circle-
      down"></span></a></p>
  </div>
</section>
```

At present, with only default Bootstrap styles in place, the result looks like the following screenshot:

After completing the following steps, our jumbotron should look like the following screenshot:

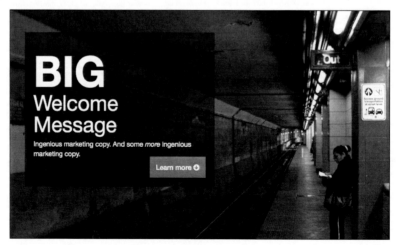

Let's start by expanding the height of our jumbotron and putting our desired background image in place:

1. Open our custom LESS file, `less/_page-content.less`, in your editor. This is the file we'll use for customizing many of the details of our page.

2. Now, let's set the height, background color, and font color for the `#welcome` section. While at it, we'll add some top margin to the button:

```
#welcome {
    height: 300px;
    background-color: #191919;
    color: #fff;
    .btn {
    margin-top: 16px;
    }
}
```

3. Save these changes and compile the file to CSS. You should see this result:

Next, let's use a media query to place our background image for medium screens and up (991px, according to the current default Bootstrap media query breakpoint values):

 If you would like, take a few minutes to open `_variables.less`, then search for and revisit Bootstrap's media query variables such as `@screen-xs`, `@screen-sm`, `@screen-md`, and `@screen-lg`.

1. We can use the power of LESS to nest a media query within the context of the `#welcome` selector. Within this media query, we'll specify the `subway-906x600.jpg` image for the background. This image is scaled to be large enough for this breakpoint while still loading relatively quickly:

```
#welcome {
    ...

    @media (max-width: @screen-sm-max) {
```

```
        background: #191919 url('../img/subway-906x600.jpg')
            center center no-repeat;
    }
}
```

2. Save the file, compile it to CSS, and refresh your browser. You should see the new background image appear—but only within a window width of 991px or less:

3. Next, let's expand the height of the jumbotron for tablet-sized viewports. We'll write a media query that uses @screen-sm-min as its breakpoint, which increases the #welcome element's height to 480px within this breakpoint:

```
@media (min-width: @screen-sm-min) {
    height: 480px;
}
```

4. Save the file, compile it to CSS, and refresh your browser. You should see the jumbotron grow to 480px in height for viewports between 768 to 991px in width, as shown in the following screenshot:

5. Now for medium and larger (greater than 992px in width) viewports, we'll increase the height of the jumbotron to 540px. At this width, we'll use the larger version of the subway-1600x1060.jpg background image. While at it, we'll set the background size to cover:

```
@media (min-width: @screen-md-min) {
    height: 540px;
    background: #191919 url('../img/subway-1600x1060.jpg')
      center center no-repeat;
    -webkit-background-size: cover;
    -moz-background-size: cover;
    -o-background-size: cover;
    background-size: cover;
}
```

6. With these style rules in place, large viewports will have a 1600px-wide background image. Modern browsers, including Internet Explorer 9 and above, will stretch the background image to fill the #welcome element.

7. Save the file, compile it to CSS, and test. You should find that we have our major breakpoints nicely covered.

 Be aware that Internet Explorer 8, when stretched beyond 1600px in width, will reveal the #191919 background color at the left and right edges. This should not affect many users; however, when it does happen, it will not be greatly distracting.

Next, we can style our big marketing message for maximum impact.

Refining the jumbotron message design

Our client wants the welcome message in the jumbotron to be extra big. Bootstrap's jumbotron styles increase the font size by 150 percent. We want to enhance the results further. We also want to constrain the width of the message on wide screens and put a dark translucent box behind it.

Our current results work well for extra-small screens:

We can, however, improve the contrast of our text by placing a translucent dark overlay behind the text. Let's do that here by performing the following steps:

1. In `index.html`, add a new `div` tag inside the jumbotron `container` class and above the `h1` heading and paragraph. Give this new `div` tag a class of `welcome-message`:

```
<section id="welcome" class="jumbotron">
  <div class="container">
    <div class="welcome-message">
      <h1><strong>Big</strong> Welcome Message</h1>
      <p>Ingenious marketing copy. And some <em>more</em>
        ingenious marketing copy.<a href="#features"
        class="btn btn-lg btn-primary pull-right">Learn
        more <span class="icon fa fa-arrow-circle-
        down"></span></a></p>
    </div><!-- /.welcome-message -->
  </div>
</section>
```

2. Now to create some styles for this new div, we will perform the following steps:

    ◦   Give it a translucent dark background using HSLA.

    ◦   Stretch it to fill the full width and height of our jumbotron by positioning it as `absolute` and setting its top, bottom, left, and right values to `0`.

- ○ Position the jumbotron itself as `relative` using the `welcome` ID so that it will anchor our absolute-positioned welcome message.
- ○ Add internal padding to the welcome message.
- ○ Use the provided `strong` tag to transform the word **Big** to uppercase and increase its font size.

```
#welcome {
    ...
    position: relative;
    .welcome-message {
    background-color: hsla(0,0,1%,0.4);
    position: absolute;
    top: 0;
    bottom: 0;
        left: 0;
    right: 0;
    padding: 30px 40px;
        strong {
            font-size: 1.5em;
            text-transform: uppercase
        }
    }
    ...
}
```

3. Save the file, compile it to CSS, and refresh your browser. You should see the background darken and the text stand out more clearly against it, as shown in the following screenshot:

4. Next, we can address the `@screen-sm` breakpoint. We've already written a media query for this breakpoint in order to increase the jumbotron height to 480px. Within this same breakpoint, we can add rules to do the following:

   ○ Position the container as `relative` to make it our new anchor point, which will push our welcome message away from the top and left edges

   ○ Push the right edge 20 percent from the right

   ○ Set the bottom edge to `auto` so that it can stretch to fit our content

   ○ Set the word **Big** to display block and fill its own line

```
@media (min-width: @screen-sm-min) {
    height: 480px;
    .container {
      position: relative;
    }
    .welcome-message {
      right: 20%;
      bottom: auto;
      strong {
        display: block;
      }
    }
}
```

5. Save the file, compile it to CSS, and refresh your browser. You should see the following result:

6. Finally, let's address the medium and large viewports. We'll constrain the width a bit more. This can all be done under the previously created `@screen-md-min` media query:

```
@media (min-width: @screen-md-min) {
    ...
    .welcome-message {
    right: 50%;
    }
}
```

7. Save the file, compile it to CSS, and refresh your browser. You should see the following result in a medium viewport:

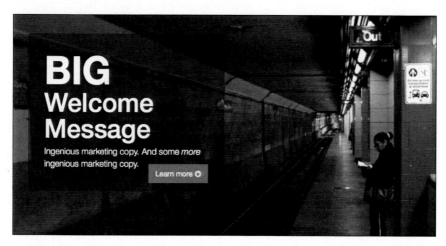

Mission accomplished!

Our customized jumbotron is finished, providing the large welcome message our client has asked for including the ability to adapt to tablet- and phone-sized viewports, which we've accomplished efficiently with a mobile-first approach.

Now we're ready to move on to the features list.

Beautifying the features list

With icons, titles, and short descriptions, our features section currently looks like the following screenshot in a wide viewport:

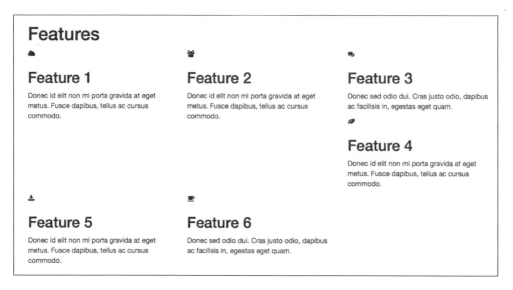

We need to enlarge the icons, align the text at the center, and iron out the grid layout.

Let's review the markup structure for the features list:

```
<section id="features">
  <div class="container">
    <h1>Features</h1>
    <div class="row">
      <div class="features-item col-md-4">
        <span class="icon fa fa-cloud"></span>
        <h2>Feature 1</h2>
        <p>Donec id elit non mi porta gravida at eget metus. Fusce
          dapibus, tellus ac cursus commodo. </p>
      </div>
      ...
```

 Each feature with its icon, heading, and paragraph is wrapped in a div tag with two classes: `features-item` and `col-md-4`.

With this in mind, let's write the styles we need:

1. With `_page-contents.less` opened in your editor, add a new section with a comment for our `#features` section.

    ```less
    // Features Section
    #features {


    }
    ```

2. Now let's focus on the `.features-item` section by aligning the text at the center, adding padding, providing a set height to keep the floating items from interfering with each other, and increasing the `.icon` font size to 90px:

    ```less
    #features {
        .features-item {
        text-align: center;
        padding: 20px;
        height: 270px;
        .icon {
          font-size: 90px;
        }
          }
    }
    ```

3. Save the file, compile it to CSS, and refresh the browser. You should see the following result in a medium viewport:

    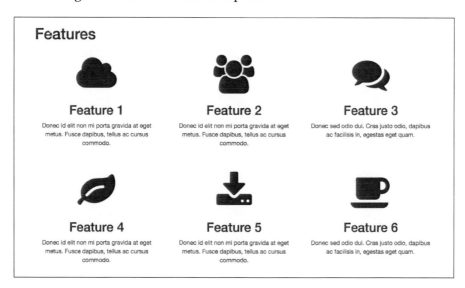

That's a great start!

4. Now let's adapt our features section for small screens. Currently, our `.features-item` section includes a class of `col-md-4`. We can shift our small-screen layout to two columns as shown in the following screenshot by adding a class of `col-sm-6`:

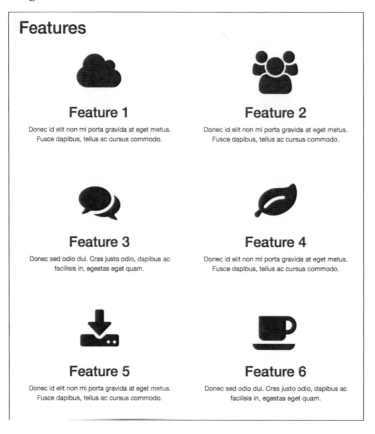

5. And then, of course, they'll arrange themselves in a single column for extra-small screens.

6. Unfortunately, at the upper range of extra-small screens, 500px to 767px, the full-width layout allows the descriptive text to range too wide.

7. We can fix this by adding a media query within which we set a maximum width on the `.features-item` section and apply Bootstrap's `.center-block()` mixin:

```
#features {
    .features-item {
        ...
        @media (max-width: @screen-xs-max) {
            max-width: 320px;
            .center-block();
        }
    }
}
```

 The `.center-block()` mixin is found in the `mixins.less` file in the `bootstrap` folder. It applies `auto` left and right margin to the element.

8. With these lines in place, our `.features-item` elements retain their desired dimensions across all viewports!

At this point, we have satisfied our client's demands for this section of her website! We're ready to move on to the customer reviews.

Tackling customer reviews

Our next section, named **Impact**, presents reviews from happy customers. In this section, we see smiling faces of happy customers with excerpts of their commentary about our client's product. The initial markup starts as follows:

```
<!-- IMPACT SECTION -->
<section id="impact">
  <div class="container">
  <h1>Impact</h1>
    <div class="reviews">
```

Each review is marked up as follows using the `hreview` microformat:

```
<div class="hreview review-item-1 thumbnail">
  <img src="img/smiling1-by-RomainGuy-600x900.jpg" alt="Customer
Photo1">
  <div class="caption">
    <blockquote class="description"><p>Lorem ipsum dolor sit amet,
consectetur adipiscing elit. Proin euismod, nulla pretium commodo
ultricies</p></blockquote>
    <p class="reviewer">Smiling Customer1</p>
  </div><!-- /.caption -->
</div><!-- /.hreview -->
```

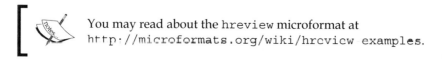

You may read about the `hreview` microformat at `http://microformats.org/wiki/hreview examples`.

For purposes of layout and style, we've employed Bootstrap's thumbnail class structure. This structure offers us the following benefits:

- For the parent element of each review, we've added the `thumbnail` class alongside the `hreview` class

- The review content, including both the quoted text and the reviewer's name, is wrapped in `div class="caption"`

This thumbnail and caption structure provides an overall wrapper for each review. Bootstrap's thumbnail styles are designed to constrain the proportions of images and captions within our desired layout.

Both in terms of semantics and presentational starting points, we're off to a good start.

Because we want to arrive at a masonry layout, our images are a mixture of portrait and landscape aspect ratios. We've made them all of equal width in order to provide enough room for bright faces and textual overlays with short laudatory statements.

Without Bootstrap layout classes, the images simply flow vertically, one after another. If you constrain your window width to a value approximately in the range of 320 to 400px, you can see how they will look as one narrow vertical column, as shown in the following screenshot:

Before addressing the layout for larger viewports, let's start by tackling the captions.

Positioning and styling the captions

Let's begin by positioning our captions as overlays atop their respective customer photos:

1. While editing the `_page-contents.less` file, add a new comment and selector for the `#impact` section:

   ```less
   // Impact Section
   #impact {

   }
   ```

2. Now let's add styles to set the necessary context for each `.hreview` class element. We'll apply relative positioning, add padding, and remove the default Bootstrap thumbnail border:

   ```less
   #impact {
     .hreview {
       position: relative;
       padding: 0 10px;
       border: none;
     }
   }
   ```

3. Now, we can work on the captions. We'll add a translucent background and position them as `absolute` at the bottom of each image:

   ```less
   .hreview {
     ...
     .caption {
       position: absolute;
       top: auto;
       left: 10px;
       right: 10px;
       bottom: 0;
       line-height: 1.1;
       background: hsla(0,0,10%,0.55);
     }
   ```

4. Next, we'll strip away the unnecessary margin and padding from the blockquote and `.reviewer` elements, specifying just what we need:

   ```less
   #impact .hreview {
     ...
     .caption {
       ...
       blockquote,
       .reviewer {
   ```

```
    margin: 0 6px;
    padding: 0;
}
```

5. Now, we can focus on the review text and specify the margin, border, font family, font size, and color:

```
blockquote {
    margin-top: 4px;
    border: none;
    font-family: @font-family-serif;
    font-size: @font-size-large;
    color: #fff;
}
```

6. Next, specify styles for the reviewer's name, which appears below the review text:

```
...
.reviewer {
    margin-top: 2px;
    margin-bottom: 4px;
    text-align: right;
    color: @gray-lighter;
}
```

 Be sure to close each set of curly braces.

7. Save the file, compile it to CSS, refresh the browser, and check your progress.

Lorem ipsum dolor sit amet, consectetur adipiscing elit. Proin euismod, nulla pretium commodo ultricies

Smiling Customer1

Scroll down and see how the results look in the other review items.

Not bad! However, we can do it one step better.

Refining the caption position

Looking carefully at the available open space in the preceding images and examining the overlap variations at various viewport widths in your responsive grid, you may want to position each caption in a way that works best for each customer's photo.

This is where the `review-item-1`, `review-item-2`, and so on classes become relevant and helpful, as we may use these specific classes to position each caption in a way that fits best with its image. I've added the following lines in the `_page-contents.less` file:

```
#impact {
  .review-item-4 .caption {
    top: 0;
    left: 62%;
    right: 10px;
    bottom: auto;
```

```
     .reviewer {
       margin-top: 6px;
       text-align: left;
     }
   }
   .review-item-5 .caption {
     top: 0;
     left: 17%;
     right: 10px;
     bottom: auto;
   }
 }
```

The preceding markup adjusts the absolute positioning of each specific caption, which yields results as shown in the following screenshot:

You'll see that I've applied specific positioning values from lines 132 and onwards in the `less/_page-contents.less` file in the `06_Code_END` folder in this chapter's exercise files. As you survey the results, you may disagree with my judgment calls—about positioning, styling, or both. That's fine. Take over and fine-tune from here!

Meanwhile, let's move on toward our masonry layout. The first step will be to specify the widths of our elements. Let's utilize Bootstrap's grid classes for this.

Adding Bootstrap grid classes

By utilizing Bootstrap's responsive grid classes, we can prepare a two-column layout for small screens using the `col-sm-6` class. For medium screens and up, we can shift to a three-column layout using the `col-md-4` class.

The resulting class structure for each `hreview` element will look like the following line:

```
<div class="hreview review-item-1 thumbnail col-sm-6 col-md-4">
```

Add these two column classes to each review item.

Save the file, refresh your browser, and expand your window across the small and medium breakpoints. You'll see a result similar to the following screenshot for small viewports:

For medium viewports and higher, you'll see a result similar to the following screenshot:

In the features section discussed earlier, we discovered that when we have grid items of varying heights, they bump into one another and do not automatically create a cohesive grid. We fixed this by giving each element a set height value. But in this section, we want our items to have varying heights. We want a masonry layout, and this requires a bit of JavaScript.

Downloading and linking up the Masonry JavaScript plugin

A masonry layout utilizes JavaScript to assess available spaces and fill those spaces with the elements that fit them best, with the goal of producing nicely tiled columns from building blocks of varying heights.

To implement masonry in this design, we'll utilize the excellent JavaScript plugin named Masonry, which has been developed and maintained by David DeSandro:

1. In your browser, navigate to `http://masonry.desandro.com`.
2. Download the minified, production-ready file `masonry.pkgd.min.js`.
3. Open `masonry.pkgd.min.js` in your editor and copy its entire contents.
4. Now, in your project files, open `js/plugins.js`. Paste the masonry code with its opening comments just after the end of Bootstrap's JavaScript lines.
5. Save and close the file.

Recall that the `plugins.js` file is already linked to your `index.html` file. Similarly, we've added masonry to our page's available scripts! (While we've added some file size, we have not added any new HTTP requests.)

Initializing Masonry JavaScript on our reviews layout

We'll now initialize masonry in our page using HTML attributes.

 For Masonry documentation, check `http://masonry.desandro.com/#getting-started`.

In the `index.html` file, perform the following steps:

1. Add the `js-masonry` class to `div class="reviews"`, which is the parent of all of our review items. This lets masonry know where to do its work.
2. Then, on the same element, add a data attribute to specify the masonry items. The resulting tag should look like the following line:

```
<div class="reviews js-masonry" data-masonry-
    options='{"itemSelector": ".hreview" }'>
```

It's important that the `data-masonry-options` attribute uses single and double quotes in exactly the following pattern: `data-masonry-options='{ "itemSelector": ".hreview" }'`.

This tells masonry which elements to arrange in the masonry layout. We've specified the `hreview` class (though we could have used `thumbnail`).

3. Save `index.html` and refresh your browser. You can see that the gaps that existed earlier disappeared as soon as the masonry filled them in.

The result for a small viewport (for which we've specified a two-column layout using `col-sm-6`) is shown in the following screenshot:

And the following is the result in a medium or large viewport:

Take a geek break by resizing your browser window back and forth across the small and medium breakpoints. Watch the review items reorganize themselves into two or three columns with the animation provided by `Masonry.js`!

Cutting and trimming our bricks

We're very close to accomplishing our client's desired result. However, one of our remaining problems is that we've possibly mismeasured the size of our images. In a small two-column layout, the image that says **Smiling Customer5** sticks out just a bit. In the medium and large three-column layout, the image sticks out even more. We could take the image out, but the review of the customer in that image is one of our client's favorites, and she loves this image. So, we're going to make this image fit properly in the viewport.

Thankfully, we have been given permission to do some trimming. And if push comes to shove, other customers are expendable. This gives us something to work with. Let's begin by fixing the three-column layout:

1. With `_page-contents.less` open in your editor, begin a new section with a comment at the top:

   ```
   // Cutting and trimming for masonry layout
   ```

2. Next, we'll make multiple adjustments at multiple breakpoints. Instead of starting with a media query, let's take advantage of the power of LESS and nest our media queries within the context of our `#impact` section. Within the first query, we'll remove the image that says **Smiling Customer4** from the layout, as shown in the following lines of code:

   ```
   #impact {
     @media (min-width: @screen-md-min) {
       .review-item-4 {
         display: none;
       }
     }
   }
   ```

3. Save the file, compile it to CSS, and refresh your browser. Your three-column layout should now be nicely lined up! The following screenshot shows the result:

Now let's adjust the image in the two-column layout.

 The image that says **Smiling Customer5** sticks out perhaps 20px below the others. What's needed here is to trim the photo a little by slicing some pixels from the bottom edge.

We need to slice these pixels only for the small layout—not extra-small and not medium or large. Thus, we'll need both minimum and maximum values in our media query. Adding this media query below the first query, we can accomplish our goals as shown in the following lines of code:

```
@media (min-width: @screen-sm-min) and (max-width: @screen-sm-max) {
    .review-item-5 {
      height: 474px;
      overflow: hidden;
      img {
        width: 100%;
      }
    }
  }
```

By adding these lines, we have performed the following:

- Set the height of the `review-item-5` div to precisely 474 pixels so that it will share the same bottom edge with its neighboring item
- Hidden the overflow, cutting off the bottom portion of the image from the view
- Forced the image to fill the width of its available space so that it keeps its needed width

The result works nicely! The following screenshot shows the desired result:

We're looking great!

Adjusting for tiny screens

It seems that Bootstrap's responsive grid and masonry's layout magic has combined to form a nasty concoction for tiny viewports—at least in some browsers. In my browser, images grow huge and no longer stay constrained.

This is because Bootstrap's `col-sm-` and `col-lg-` classes no longer apply at this tiny dimension. As a result, our `hreview` thumbnails and their images have gone completely unconstrained by any specification of width.

At this point, we could do one of the following two things:

- Go back and add `col-12` to each review item
- Set our own constraints with a little custom LESS

The choice is up to you. As for me, at this point in the flow of things, I'd rather take the second option.

To do so, I'll simply add one more media query in the `_page-contents.less` file:

```
@media (max-width: @screen-xs-max) {
```

Within this media query, let's limit the `max-width` property of `div class="reviews"` to 400px—a width that leaves our images large enough without allowing them to expand too large. Then, let's use the `.center-block()` mixin to center align the reviews using `auto` left and right margins as shown in the following lines of code:

```
#impact {
    @media (max-width: @screen-xs-max) {
      .reviews {
    max-width: 400px;
      .center-block();
      }
    }
}
```

Save the file and then refresh your browser.

Voila! The customer reviews are now performing exactly according to our client's desires.

Now to take care of the last major item in our client's desired home page design: the pricing tables.

Creating attention-grabbing pricing tables

Let's revisit the mockup of how our client would like the pricing tables to look on desktop-sized screens:

Let's see how close we can get to the desired result, and what we can work out for other viewport sizes.

Setting up the variables, files, and markup

As shown in the preceding screenshot, there are a few tables in this design. We can begin by adjusting a few fundamental variables for all tables. These are found in `_variables.less`. Search for the tables section and adjust the variables for background, accented rows, and borders as desired. I've made these adjustments as shown in the following lines of code:

```
// Tables
// -------------------------
...
@table-bg:          transparent; // overall background-color
@table-bg-accent:   hsla(0,0,1%,.1); // for striping
@table-bg-hover:    hsla(0,0,1%,.2);
@table-bg-active:   @table-bg-hover;
@table-border-color: #ccc; // table and cell border
```

Save the file, compile it to CSS, and refresh to see the result as shown in the following screenshot:

Sign up now!

Basic Plan		Premium Plan		Pro Plan	
$19		$29		$39	
Feature	Name	Feature	Name	Feature	Name
Feature	Name	Feature	Name	Feature	Name
Feature	Name	Feature	Name	Feature	Name
Feature	Name	Feature	Name	Feature	Name
Feature	Name	Feature	Name	Feature	Name
Sign up now!		Sign up now!		Sign up now!	

That's a start. Now we need to write the more specific styles.

The _page-contents.less file is now growing long, and the task before us is extensive and highly focused on table styles. To carry the custom styles, let's create a new LESS file for these pricing tables:

1. Create _pricing-tables.less in the main less folder.

2. Import it into __main.less just after _page-contents.less as shown in the following line:

   ```
   @import "_pricing-tables.less";
   ```

3. Open _pricing-tables.less in your editor and begin writing your new styles.

But before we begin writing styles, let's review the markup that we'll be working with.

We have the following special classes already provided in the markup on the parent element of each respective table:

* package package-basic
* package package-premium
* package package-pro

Thus, for the first table, you'll see the following markup on its parent `div`:

```
<div class="package package-basic col-lg-4">
  <table class="table table-striped">
...
```

Similarly, we'll use `package package-premium` and `package package-pro` for the second and third table, respectively.

These parent containers obviously also provide basic layout instructions using the `col-md-4` class to set up a three-column layout in medium viewports.

Next, we will observe the markup for each table. We see that the basic `table` and `table-striped` classes have been applied:

```
<table class="table table-striped">
```

The table uses the `<thead>` element for its top-most block. Within this, there is `<th>` spanning two columns, with an `<h2>` heading for the package name and `<div class="price">` to markup the dollar amount:

```
<thead>
  <tr>
    <th colspan="2">
      <h2>Basic Plan</h2>
      <div class="price">$19</div>
    </th>
  </tr>
</thead>
```

Next is the `tfoot` tag with the **Sign up Now!** button:

```
<tfoot>
  <tr><td colspan="2"><a href="#" class="btn">Sign up
    now!</a></td></tr>
</tfoot>
```

Then is the `tbody` tag with the list of features laid out in a straightforward manner in rows with two columns:

```
<tbody>
  <tr><td>Feature</td><td>Name</td></tr>
  <tr><td>Feature</td><td>Name</td></tr>
  <tr><td>Feature</td><td>Name</td></tr>
  <tr><td>Feature</td><td>Name</td></tr>
  <tr><td>Feature</td><td>Name</td></tr>
</tbody>
```

And finally, of course, the closing tags for the `table` and parent `div` tags:

```
</table>
</div><!-- /.package .package-basic -->
```

Each table repeats this basic structure.

This gives us what we need to start work!

Beautifying the table head

To beautify the `thead` element of all of our tables, we'll do the following:

- Align the text at the center
- Add a background color—for now, add a gray color that is approximately a midtone similar to the colors we'll apply to the final version
- Turn the font color white
- Convert the `h2` heading to uppercase
- Increase the size of the price table
- Add the necessary padding all around the tables

We can apply many of these touches with the following lines of code. We'll specify the `#signup` section as the context for these special table styles:

```
#signup {
  table {
    border: 1px solid @table-border-color;
    thead th {
      text-align: center;
      background-color: @gray-light;
      color: #fff;
      padding-top: 12px;
      padding-bottom: 32px;
      h2 {
        text-transform: uppercase;
      }
    }
  }
}
```

In short, we've accomplished everything except increasing the size of the price tables. We can get started on this by adding the following lines of code, which are still nested within our `#signup table` selector:

```
.price {
     font-size: 7em;
     line-height: 1;
}
```

This yields the following result:

This is close to our desired result, but we need to decrease the size of the dollar sign. To give ourselves control over that character, let's go to the markup and wrap a `span` tag around it:

```
<em class="price"><span>$</span>19</em>
```

Remember to do the same for the other two tables.

With this new bit of markup in place, we can nest this within our styles for `.price`:

```
.price {
    ...
    span {
         font-size: .5em;
         vertical-align: super;
    }
}
```

These lines reduce the dollar sign to half its size and align it at the top.

Now to recenter the result, we need to add a bit of negative margin to the parent `.price` selector:

```
.price {
  margin-left: -0.25em;
    ...
```

The following screenshot shows the result:

Styling the table body and foot

By continuing to focus on the styles that apply to all three pricing tables, let's make the following adjustments:

- Add left and right padding to the list of features
- Stretch the button to full width
- Increase the button size

We can accomplish this by adding the following rules:

```
#signup {
  table {
    ...
    tbody {
      td {
        padding-left: 16px;
        padding-right: 16px;
      }
    }
    a.btn {
      .btn-lg;
      display: block;
      width: 100%;
      background-color: @gray-light;
      color: #fff;
    }
  }
}
```

Save the file, compile it to CSS, and refresh the browser. You should see the following result:

We're now ready to add styles to differentiate our three packages.

Differentiating the packages

Let's begin by giving each package the desired color for the table head and the **Sign up now!** button. Our provided mockup uses blue for the **Basic**, green for the **Premium**, and red for the **Pro** packages. Let's prepare our color scheme by using the chosen color values in new variables for primary, secondary, and tertiary brand colors, as shown in the following lines of code:

```
@brand-primary:        #428bca;
@brand-secondary:    #5cb85c;
@brand-tertiary:     #d9534f;
```

Having set up these colors, we can efficiently apply them to the appropriate `thead` and `button` elements. We'll use the distinctive class that we applied earlier to each table's parent element, that is, `package-basic`, `package-premium`, and `package-pro`:

1. In the `less/_pricing-tables.less` file, begin a new section with a comment:

   ```
   // Pricing Table Colors
   ```

2. We'll apply the primary brand color to the `.package-basic` table using the `@brand-primary` variable; we'll try it first on the `thead th` element:

   ```
   #signup .package-basic table {
     thead th {
       background-color: @brand-primary;
     }
   }
   ```

3. Then, apply the primary brand color to the thead th element's button. Here, we'll use the .button-variant() mixin from the bootstrap/mixins.less file to efficiently apply styles to :hover and :active states. The mixin takes three parameters: color, background color, and border color. We'll define them as follows:

```
...
.btn {
   .button-variant(#fff; @brand-primary; darken(@brand-primary,
5%));
   }
}
```

4. When compiled, this concise mixin will generate styles for the button and its hover and active states!

 For a reminder of how the .button-variant() mixin works, consult bootstrap/mixins.less, where the mixin is defined, and then bootstrap/buttons.less, where it is used to define the default Bootstrap button classes.

5. Now, we need to repeat the same for our .package-premium table, this time, however, using the @brand-secondary variable:

```
#signup .package-premium table {
  thead th {
    background-color: @brand-secondary;
  }
  .btn {
    .button-variant(#fff; @brand-secondary; darken(@brand-
secondary, 5%));
  }
}
```

6. Finally, we'll apply the tertiary brand color to the .package-pro table using the @brand-tertiary variable:

```
#signup .package-pro table {
  thead th {
    background-color: @brand-tertiary;
  }
  .btn {
    .button-variant(#fff; @brand-tertiary; darken(@brand-tertiary,
5%));
  }
}
```

7. Save the file, compile it to CSS, and refresh your browser. You should see the new colors we applied to our tables.

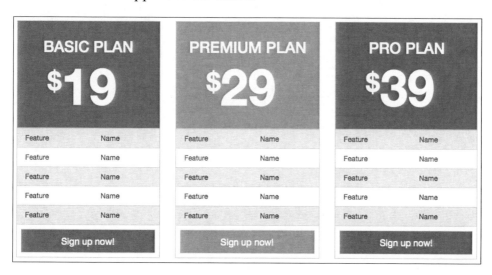

Nice!

Now, let's check how our tables respond to various viewport widths.

Adjusting for small viewports

Thanks to the attention Bootstrap 3 gives to responsive design, our tables perform quite well across viewport breakpoints. We've already seen the way our tables fair in the medium breakpoint range. In large screens, the tables expand wider, as shown in the following screenshot:

In narrow viewports, the tables stack up vertically, as shown in the following screenshot, quite nicely:

However, there is an awkward range of width approximately between 480px and 992px where the tables expand to fill the full width of the screen. Clearly, they become too wide, as shown in the following screenshot:

Because we have three tables, there is no benefit involved in having a two-column layout at this dimension. Instead, let's constrain the width of our tables and align them at the center with `auto` left and right margins. We'll use a media query with `max-width` of `@screen-sm-max` set to `400px` as our maximum width, and use the `.center-block()` mixin to keep our tables at the center in the window:

```
//
// Constrain width for small screens and under
// -----------------------------------------
```

```
@media (max-width: @screen-sm-max) {
  #signup .package {
      max-width: 400px;
      .center-block();
    }
}
```

Save the file, compile it to CSS, and refresh your browser. You should see nicely constrained tables aligned at the center within the window! The following screenshot shows our result:

At this point, our tables are differentiated by color and are responsive. However, one last step remains. In the medium and large viewport widths, we want the premium plan to stand out.

Providing visual hierarchy to our tables

If we look back at the mockup, we see that the design—at least for desktop-sized viewports—calls for visual emphasis upon the central premium plan by increasing its size and bringing it visually into the foreground, as shown in the following screenshot:

This can be accomplished with some adjustments to padding, margins, and font sizes.

We'll do this within a media query for medium viewports and up:

```
//
// Visually enhance the premium plan
// ----------------------------------------
@media (min-width: @screen-md-min) {


}
```

Nested within this media query, we can first reduce the widths of our basic and pro tables (the first and third) and add a little margin to the top to push them down a bit:

```
// Size down the basic and pro
#signup .package-basic table,
#signup .package-pro table {
  width: 90%;
  margin-top: 36px;
}
```

Next, let's enhance the font size of our premium table and add padding to its button:

```
// Size up the premium
#signup .package-premium table {
  thead th {
    font-size: 1.5em;
    h2 {
      font-size: 1.5em;
    }
  }
  a.btn {
    font-size: 2em;
    padding-top: 24px;
    padding-bottom: 24px;
  }
}
```

This already brings us very close to our desired result, as shown in the following screenshot:

Our next aim is to bring the tables closer in proximity to one another. This can be done with some margin adjustment and a bit of z-index work:

```
// Squeeze tables together
#signup .package-basic {
  margin-right: -58px;
  margin-left: 58px;
  z-index: 1;
```

```
}
#signup .package-premium {
  z-index: 1000;
}
#signup .package-pro {
  margin-left: -30px;
  z-index: 1;
}
```

Here, we have performed the following steps:

- Nudged the **BASIC PLAN** (leftmost) table to the right using a negative value for `margin-right` and compensating this by nudging the equivalent margin to the left to keep everything positioned as it was originally (else all three tables will start sliding to the left)

- Nudged the **PRO PLAN** (rightmost) table to the left with the negative left margin

- Adjusted the `z-index` values for all tables so that the basic and pro tables appear to line up behind our premium table

 For a refresher on how `z-index` works, see `http://css-tricks.com/almanac/properties/z/z-index/`.

The following screenshot is the result in a medium viewport:

Our work is almost done. We only need to adjust the margins for the basic table when we cross the next larger breakpoint. After closing the previous media query, begin a new one and add these margin adjustments:

```
@media (min-width: @screen-lg-min) {
  #signup .package-basic {
    margin-right: -65px;
    margin-left: 65px;
  }
}
```

Save the file, compile it to CSS, and refresh the browser. You should see the following result in large viewports of 1200px and above:

That's it! We've accomplished the last major challenge in our client's design.

Now, tidy things up by applying the touches that hold it all together.

Adding the final touches

In this section, we will enhance the details that hold our design together. First, we'll enhance the h1 headings for each of our major sections and add some needed top and bottom padding to each section. Then, we'll enhance the navigation experience by adding ScrollSpy to the navbar and using jQuery to animate the scrolling action when triggered by a click on the navbar item.

Let's begin by enhancing the size and contrast of our major `h1` headings for each section and increasing the top and bottom padding. If you pause to look at these `h1` headings, you may note that they are rather lackluster. Consider, for example, the heading for the **Features** section:

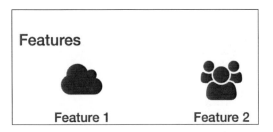

Enlarging these headings, bringing the contrast down a little, and providing extra padding will make a big difference. We only want these rules to apply to the **FEATURES**, **IMPACT**, and **SIGN UP** sections. We will select these by ID.

1. Open `_page-contents.less` in your editor.

2. At the top of the file, after the rule applying top padding to the body, add the following lines:

```
#features, #impact, #signup {
  padding-top: 36px;
  padding-bottom: 48px;
  h1 {
    font-size: 5em;
    color: @gray;
    line-height: 1.3;
    padding-bottom: 24px;
  }
}
```

3. Here, we've done the following:
   - Added the top and bottom padding to these sections
   - Significantly increased the size of the `h1` heading
   - Reduced the heavy contrast of that heading
   - Ensured that the heading has room to breathe by setting the line height and bottom padding

4. Save, compile, refresh, and notice the difference.

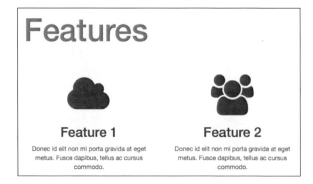

This yields a nice result across almost all viewport sizes. For small viewports, the h1 font size is now a bit large. We also need to add some left and right margins; so, let's adjust these. As we do not want these styles to flow up to larger viewports, we'll wrap them in a query by limiting them to small viewports:

```
// Adjust section headings for extra-small viewports only
@media (max-width: @screen-xs-max) {
  #features, #impact, #signup {
    margin-left: 30px;
    margin-right: 30px;
    h1 {
      font-size: 3em;
    }
  }
}
```

The following screenshot shows our result:

This is a much improved result!

Now, we'll enhance the navigation experience.

Adding ScrollSpy to the navbar

Let's configure our top navbar to indicate our location on the page. We'll add Bootstrap's ScrollSpy behavior to the navbar:

 Refer to Bootstrap's ScrollSpy plugin documentation at `http://getbootstrap.com/javascript/#scrollspy`.

1. Open `index.html` in your editor.

2. Add these ScrollSpy attributes to the `body` tag:

   ```
   <body data-spy="scroll" data-target=".navbar">
   ```

    If you include more than one navbar in a page, you will need to be more specific with the `data-target` attribute—probably giving your ScrollSpy navbar an ID such as `id="navbar-primary"` and using that for the `data-target` value instead.

3. With these new attributes in place, save the file, refresh your browser, and scroll up and down the page. You should see your main navigation respond as it should, indicating your position on the page as shown in the following screenshot:

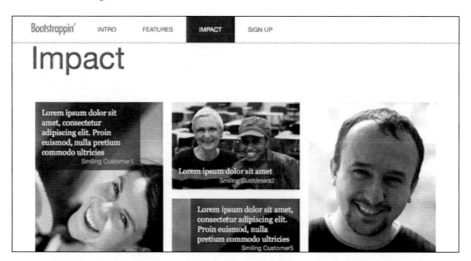

Animating the scroll

Now, let's animate the page scrolls that will be triggered by clicking on the navbar page anchors. This requires adding a few lines to our `main.js` file:

1. Open `js/main.js`.

2. Add the following lines within `$(document).ready(function() {`:

```
$('#nav-main [href^=#]').click(function (e) {
  e.preventDefault();
  var div = $(this).attr('href');
  $("html, body").animate({
    scrollTop: $(div).position().top
  }, "slow");
});
```

3. Save the file and refresh your browser.

What have we done here? We have done the following using the power of jQuery:

- Selected the links in our `.navbar` element that use page anchors as their targets

- Prevented the default click behavior

- Animated the scrolling behavior, setting its duration to slow

Click on one of the nav items and you should see it animate the scroll!

Summary

Take a moment to scroll back and forth through our page, appreciating its details and resizing it to see how it adjusts to viewport dimensions.

When we consider the variety of features packed into this page—and that they all work responsively across desktop-, tablet-, and phone-sized viewports—it's not a bad accomplishment!

To review, we have given our client a beautiful one-page marketing site with the following:

- A large welcome section using Bootstrap's jumbotron styles, a bold background image, and responsive customizations

- A features list making use of large-sized Font Awesome icons

- A section of customer reviews with images and captions laid out in the masonry format that adapts beautifully across viewports

- A signup section with custom-designed pricing tables built on Bootstrap styles and enhanced further to provide visual hierarchy for medium and large viewports

- A ScrollSpy-equipped navbar with animated scrolling behavior provided by a bit of extra jQuery

With the accomplishment of this design, we have reached a point where there is nothing we can't do with Bootstrap.

Across this and the previous projects, we have accomplished a great deal. We have:

- Learned the ins and outs of Bootstrap

- Folded Bootstrap LESS and JavaScript into our own custom set of project files

- Swapped out Bootstrap's glyphicons for the more robust Font Awesome icons

- Tweaked, customized, and otherwise innovated on Bootstrap styles to arrive precisely at the results we were seeking

Don't forget, in the appendices of this book, I have provided guidance relevant to all projects such as optimizing your Bootstrap assets for production (*Appendix A, Optimizing Site Assets*), implementing one of the current best responsive image techniques (*Appendix B, Implementing Responsive Images*), and adding swipe behavior to the carousel (*Appendix C, Adding Swipe to the Carousel*).

Beyond this, there are a plethora of resources available for pushing further with Bootstrap. The Bootstrap community is an active and exciting one. This is truly an exciting point in the history of frontend web development. Bootstrap has made a mark in history, and for a good reason.

Optimizing Site Assets

Speed matters. It matters to users. Your site has to load fast or users will leave. It matters for SEO. Your site has to load fast or search engines downgrade your ranking.

With that in mind, let's take a moment to take stock of the portfolio site in *Chapter 2, Bootstrappin' Your Portfolio*. Specifically, let's look at a key page speed factor that we can easily control, the size of our asset files—images, CSS, and JavaScript. With just a few steps, we can drastically reduce our site's footprint and improve load times.

Optimizing images

Our images have already been optimized to a degree using Photoshop's "save to web" process. But, together, they still weigh in at 856 KB.

img	--
alittlecode.jpg	149 KB
bso.jpg	169 KB
logo.png	19 KB
okwu-athletics.jpg	230 KB
okwu.jpg	267 KB

```
Kind: Folder
Size: 841,127 bytes (856 KB on disk)
      for 6 items
```

The images are important. (It's a portfolio site after all.) However, this is a considerable payload. In *Appendix B, Implementing Responsive Images*, I recommend a responsive image technique that will reduce the file size for smaller devices. But even without that technique, if we can reduce the file size by compressing these files more effectively, we should do it.

We can usually squeeze out a few more pixels without damaging our images by using tools such as Yahoo!'s Smushit (`http://www.smushit.com/`).

For Mac users, the free ImageOptim app at `http://imageoptim.com/` is a similarly helpful tool. By using it in this case, I've been able to shave a total of 29 KB off my combined image weight.

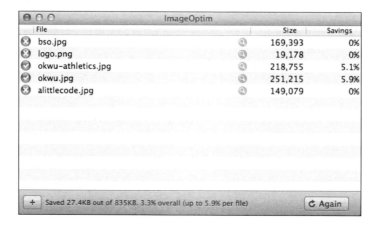

That's not a gigantic gain, but every bit helps a little. Let's keep going.

Optimizing CSS

Check out the size of our unoptimized stylesheet, `main.css`:

It's 137 KB! No conscientious developer should ship such a gigantic stylesheet for so small a website.

Thankfully, we can easily cut the size of this file by nearly half. We'll use the power of Bootstrap's modular LESS organization to quickly cut it down to size. Here's how:

1. Open `less/__main.less`.

2. Comment out all unnecessary LESS files, such as these:

   ```
   // @import "bootstrap/glyphicons.less";
   ...
   // @import "bootstrap/dropdowns.less";
   // @import "bootstrap/button-groups.less";
   // @import "bootstrap/input-groups.less";
   ```

```
. . .
// @import "bootstrap/breadcrumbs.less";
// @import "bootstrap/pagination.less";
// @import "bootstrap/pager.less";
// @import "bootstrap/labels.less";
// @import "bootstrap/badges.less";
// @import "bootstrap/jumbotron.less";
// @import "bootstrap/thumbnails.less";
// @import "bootstrap/alerts.less";
// @import "bootstrap/progress-bars.less";
// @import "bootstrap/media.less";
// @import "bootstrap/list-group.less";
// @import "bootstrap/panels.less";
// @import "bootstrap/wells.less";
// @import "bootstrap/close.less";

. . .
// @import "bootstrap/modals.less";
// @import "bootstrap/tooltip.less";
// @import "bootstrap/popovers.less";
```

3. You'll need to be careful, of course. You may inadvertently eliminate a necessary file. Take time to recompile and test thoroughly.

4. Once done, set your compiler to minify and/or to compress its output, and then recompile one last time to `css/main.css`.

5. Check out the new file size. My resulting file weighs in at only 74 KB, which is 62 percent of its original size.

Of course, you can press further. You could, for example, take a bit more time, open each of your remaining `.less` files, and comment out the lines within each one. I'll leave that step to you.

Finally, let's get to the JavaScript.

Optimizing JavaScript

Here, we will replace the Bootstrap plugins in our `plugins.js` file with only the specific Bootstrap plugins we need. Then, we'll compress the file.

1. Open `js/plugins.js`.

2. Remove the block of code belonging to `bootstrap.min.js`.

3. In our js/bootstrap folder, recall that we've kept the Bootstrap plugins as distinct files. Open each of the following three plugins and copy and paste the code from each into our plugins.js file. These are the only Bootstrap plugins we're using for this design:

   ○ carousel.js

   ○ collapse.js

   ○ transition.js

4. Save your new, slimmer plugins.js file. Refresh your browser and test it:

   ○ Make sure that your responsive navbar collapses for narrow viewports and drops down when the button is clicked.

   ○ Make sure your carousel runs as it should.

   If these things are working, we've got the JavaScript we need.

5. We're now ready to minify and/or uglify the plugins.js file. A few free and convenient online tools include the following:

   ○ UglifyJS JavaScript minification (http://marijnhaverbeke.nl/uglifyjs)

   ○ The YUI Compressor (http://refresh-sf.com/yui/)

   ○ Google's Closure Compiler (http://closure-compiler.appspot.com/)

   With these tools, you can copy the contents of plugins.js, paste it into the online interface, run the compressor, and copy the code back into plugins.js.

   For this exercise, I used CodeKit, a premium app for Mac (http://incident57.com/codekit/).

6. Save the file.

7. Compare the file size.

I've kept copies of my files as follows:

- plugins-all.js contains the entire bootstrap.min.js

- plugins-uncompressed.js contains just the three needed plugins, uncompressed

- plugins.js is the final file, minified and concatenated

You can see the results in this screenshot:

📄	plugins–all.js	28 KB
📄	plugins–uncompressed.js	14 KB
📄	plugins.js	8 KB

The final file is less than one-third the size of the original!

Our optimized results

Cumulatively, our efforts have made a difference. Between the images, CSS, and JavaScript, our original site payload was 1021 KB.

After our optimization efforts, we've cut it down to 909 KB—a saving of 112 KB or over 10 percent reduction in our total site footprint.

If we focus on the CSS and JavaScript file sizes, it's over a 50 percent saving. That's a huge difference. Chances are that it will be noticed.

We can improve things further, especially for small devices, by implementing a solid responsive images technique. For that, let me point you to *Appendix B, Implementing Responsive Images*.

B

Implementing Responsive Images

If our workflow is to be truly mobile friendly, we need a good responsive image technique. In this exercise, we'll implement one of the current leading techniques to improve both the performance and the design of the portfolio carousel implemented in *Chapter 2, Bootstrappin' Your Portfolio*.

Considering our portfolio carousel

If you recall from *Chapter 2, Bootstrappin' Your Portfolio*, the carousel images are crafted to fill a full-width layout. The images are 1,600 pixels wide and weigh in between 135 to 189 KB. To send these same images to phones and small non-retina tablets is overkill. In an age of mobile-first responsive design, it's irresponsible.

Furthermore, if you stop and look at the design on a narrow viewport, you may realize that your carousel would look better if the images were a bit taller and narrower, allowing them to fill more of the vertical space we have available on a narrow screen.

At a phone-width viewport, our images—which are crafted for wide screens—may work, but they would work better if they made use of more of our available vertical space. This can be seen in the following screenshot:

A good responsive images technique will allow us to provide exactly the images we need for narrow viewports, answering the need for smaller file sizes and quicker load times as well as improved design.

Choosing a solution from the available solutions

The quest for a standards-based approach to responsive images is underway. However, no solution has yet been adopted, nor has any consistent approach been implemented by browser vendors. For that reason, the best current techniques rely on server-side or client-side solutions.

Smashing Magazine has recently published a good article named *Choosing a Responsive Image Solution*, by *Sherri Alexander*, summarizing some leading current options. You can review the article at `http://mobile.smashingmagazine.com/2013/07/08/choosing-a-responsive-image-solution/`.

In this and other reviews, Scott Jehl's Picturefill technique consistently emerges as a leading contender. This is because the Picturefill solution admirably addresses problems of both performance and design. And it does so rather elegantly.

The approach requires just a few steps, as follows:

1. Prepare optimal images for your targeted viewports.
2. Download and include the Picturefill JavaScript.
3. Employ the Picturefill markup pattern for your images.

As always, there are two additional steps to any development process, as follows:

- Test
- Adjust as required

Let's walk through the steps together.

Preparing our responsive images

If you look in the exercise files for this appendix, I've provided a set of specially sized and optimized images in the `img` folder. You'll see these named with a `-sm.jpg` suffix.

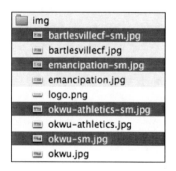

If you view these images, you'll see that they are cropped narrower and have a somewhat taller aspect ratio, filling more vertical space on a narrow viewport as shown in the following image:

The images are also smaller. They measure 900 x 600px, still enough to provide decent pixel density to a retina screen, but much less than the original 1600 x 800px images. And the smaller images average approximately 50 percent of the file size.

Note the comparatively smaller file sizes of the images ending with -sm.jpg in the following screenshot:

bartlesvillecf-sm.jpg	71 KB
bartlesvillecf.jpg	135 KB
emancipation-sm.jpg	78 KB
emancipation.jpg	156 KB
logo.png	19 KB
okwu-athletics-sm.jpg	94 KB
okwu-athletics.jpg	189 KB
okwu-sm.jpg	93 KB
okwu.jpg	188 KB

With our images ready and in place, it's time to grab the JavaScript.

Plugging in the JavaScript

The Picturefill files and documentation are hosted at GitHub at `https://github.com/scottjehl/picturefill`.

Take a few minutes to read the documentation. We'll soon be using elements recommended there. For now, we need to grab the JavaScript and include it in our project files. So, perform the following steps:

1. At the Picturefill GitHub repository, download the files or click through them and find the `picturefill.js` file.

2. Copy the code, including the opening comment. We need to copy it to our `plugins.js` file.

3. In our project files, open `js/plugins.js` and paste the Picturefill code either before or after the code for our other plugins.

4. Save. (And of course, remember to minify and compress `plugins.js` before going to production.)

Now, let's implement the Picturefill markup structure.

Implementing the markup structure

In `index.html`, we'll update the markup for each image using Picturefill's pattern of nested span elements. We'll structure it to provide the smaller images by default, except for browsers with viewports 640px wide or larger and Internet Explorer 8.

The following is the markup pattern for the structure, as implemented for the first image:

```
<span data-picture data-alt="OKWU Homepage">
  <span data-src="img/okwu-sm.jpg"></span>
  <span data-src="img/okwu.jpg" data-media="(min-width:
    640px)"></span>
  <!--[if (lt IE 9) & (!IEMobile)]>
    <span data-src="img/okwu.jpg"></span>
  <![endif]-->
  <noscript>
    <img src="img/okwu.jpg" alt="OKWU Athletics Homepage">
  </noscript>
</span>
```

Let me give you a quick overview of how the preceding code works:

- The top-level span tag identifies the entire element as a responsive image using the data-picture attribute.

- The data-alt attribute provides the alt text for the image.

- The initial <span data-src ...> tag specifies the default image to be used for smaller devices.

- The data-media attribute allows us to specify under what conditions the larger version of the image is to be used. In our case, we've specified min-width: 640px so that window screens wider than 640px will load the larger image.

 As explained in the documentation, you may use compound media queries as well as queries for pixel ratio to target high-density or retina screens.

- The conditional comment ensures that Internet Explorer 8, which does not support media queries, receives the larger image size, as it should.

- The no-script element provides a standard image tag that will be used only in cases where a browser is not running JavaScript.

For further insight, review the documentation found at https://github.com/scottjehl/picturefill.

Now, be sure to update the markup for the other three images using the same pattern.

Testing and adjusting

If you save and test, you may notice that the carousel images no longer adjust to fit the width of the carousel. This is because the Picturefill markup pattern throws off the selectors used in Bootstrap's carousel styles.

We need to update one selector group in the _carousel.less file to ensure our images adapt to their available space, as follows:

1. Open _carousel.less.

2. Search for the following section of code. Replace the > img and > a > img child selectors with a simple descendant img selector so that it will successfully select the images that are now nested deeper in our Picturefill markup:

```
// Account for jankitude on images
// > img, // commented out
// > a > img // commented out
```

```
img { // added to apply to PictureFill responsive image
    solution
    .img-responsive();
    line-height: 1;
    min-width: 100%; // added
    height: auto; // added
}
```

That should take care of it!

Our end results

On viewports below 640px, your new carousel should now use the smaller, taller, more narrowly cropped version of the images.

From here, you may consult the documentation and adjust and adapt your own version of this approach as required.

C
Adding Swipe to the Carousel

On touch-enabled devices, the ability to swipe through a carousel offers a significant usability benefit. In this exercise, we will add swipe interaction to the Bootstrap carousel.

Considering our options

Currently, there is no foolproof way to test for touch across devices. A best practice under present circumstances is to add touch events when there is a usability gain and when we can do it without conflicting with our standard mouse events. In our case, we can easily enable swipe events on our home page carousel with a JavaScript plugin and a few lines of code.

Justin Lazanowski has posted a nice write-up of three easy options for implementing swipe interaction for the Bootstrap 3 carousel. Read his post at `http://lazcreative.com/blog/adding-swipe-support-to-bootstrap-carousel-3-0/`.

We'll go with the TouchSwipe jQuery plugin hosted on GitHub at `https://github.com/mattbryson/TouchSwipe-Jquery-Plugin`.

By this route, we can add swipe interaction to our carousel with the following two steps:

1. Fold the TouchSwipe plugin into our `plugins` file.
2. Add a few lines to our `main.js` file.

It's that simple. Let's do it.

Getting and including the TouchSwipe plugin

Let's add `TouchSwipe.js` to our plugins file:

1. Go to the TouchSwipe GitHub repository at `https://github.com/mattbryson/TouchSwipe-Jquery-Plugin`.

2. Download the repository.

3. Find the `jquery.touchSwipe.min.js` file and copy the code.

4. Paste the plugin code into your `plugins.js` file in the `js` folder after the Bootstrap plugins.

5. Save the file.

Plugin added. Now let's initialize it.

Initializing TouchSwipe

With just a few lines, we can direct TouchSwipe to detect swipe events on the carousel and translate them into the Bootstrap methods: `.carousel('prev')` and `.carousel('next')`. See these methods referenced in the Bootstrap documentation at `http://getbootstrap.com/javascript/#carousel`.

If you'd like to, you may also consult the TouchSwipe documentation at `http://labs.rampinteractive.co.uk/touchSwipe`.

Our present task is very straightforward, as shown in the following steps:

1. In your project files, open `main.js` in the `js` folder

2. Add the following lines of code in the opened file:

```
//Enable swiping...
$(".carousel-inner").swipe( {
  //Generic swipe handler for all directions
  swipeRight:function(event, direction, distance, duration,
    fingerCount) {
    $(this).parent().carousel('prev');
  },
  swipeLeft: function() {
    $(this).parent().carousel('next');
  },
  //Default is 75px, set to 0 so any distance triggers swipe
  threshold:0
});
```

3. Save the file.

Now, if you test these files on a touch device, you should be able to swipe left to go to the next slide and right to go to the previous one.

That's it. It's a small cost with a clear usability gain.

Congratulations! Your Bootstrap carousel is now swipe enabled.

Index

Thank you for buying
Bootstrap Site Blueprints

About Packt Publishing

Packt, pronounced 'packed', published its first book "*Mastering phpMyAdmin for Effective MySQL Management*" in April 2004 and subsequently continued to specialize in publishing highly focused books on specific technologies and solutions.

Our books and publications share the experiences of your fellow IT professionals in adapting and customizing today's systems, applications, and frameworks. Our solution based books give you the knowledge and power to customize the software and technologies you're using to get the job done. Packt books are more specific and less general than the IT books you have seen in the past. Our unique business model allows us to bring you more focused information, giving you more of what you need to know, and less of what you don't.

Packt is a modern, yet unique publishing company, which focuses on producing quality, cutting-edge books for communities of developers, administrators, and newbies alike. For more information, please visit our website: www.packtpub.com.

About Packt Open Source

In 2010, Packt launched two new brands, Packt Open Source and Packt Enterprise, in order to continue its focus on specialization. This book is part of the Packt Open Source brand, home to books published on software built around Open Source licenses, and offering information to anybody from advanced developers to budding web designers. The Open Source brand also runs Packt's Open Source Royalty Scheme, by which Packt gives a royalty to each Open Source project about whose software a book is sold.

Writing for Packt

We welcome all inquiries from people who are interested in authoring. Book proposals should be sent to author@packtpub.com. If your book idea is still at an early stage and you would like to discuss it first before writing a formal book proposal, contact us; one of our commissioning editors will get in touch with you.

We're not just looking for published authors; if you have strong technical skills but no writing experience, our experienced editors can help you develop a writing career, or simply get some additional reward for your expertise.

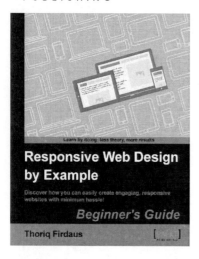

Responsive Web Design by Example Beginner's Guide

ISBN: 978-1-84969-542-8   Paperback: 338 pages

Discover how you can easily create engaging, responsive websites with minimum hassle!

1. Rapidly develop and prototype responsive websites by utilizing powerful open source frameworks.

2. Focus less on the theory and more on results, with clear step-by-step instructions, previews, and examples to help you along the way.

3. Learn how you can utilize three of the most powerful responsive frameworks available today: Bootstrap, Skeleton, and Zurb Foundation.

HTML5 and CSS3 Responsive Web Design Cookbook

ISBN: 978-1-84969-544-2   Paperback: 204 pages

Learn the secrets of developing responsive websites capable of interfacing with today's mobile Internet devices

1. Learn the fundamental elements of writing responsive website code for all stages of the development lifecycle.

2. Create the ultimate code writer's resource using logical workflow layers.

3. Full of usable code for immediate use in your website projects.

4. Written in an easy-to-understand language giving knowledge without preaching.

Please check **www.PacktPub.com** for information on our titles

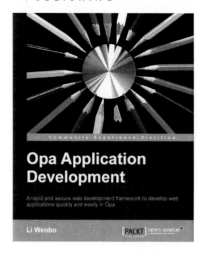

Opa Application Development

ISBN: 978-1-78216-374-9   Paperback: 116 pages

A rapid and secure web development framework to develop web applications quickly and easily in Opa

1. Discover the Opa framework in a progressive and structured way.

2. Build secure, powerful web applications with Opa.

3. Create three complete web application demos with Opa.

HTML5 Boilerplate Web Development

ISBN: 978-1-84951-850-5   Paperback: 174 pages

Master Web Development with a robust set of templates to get your projects done quickly and effectively

1. Master HTML5 Boilerplate as starting templates for future projects.

2. Learn how to optimize your workflow with HTML5 Boilerplate templates and set up servers optimized for performance.

3. Learn to feature-detect and serve appropriate styles and scripts across browser types.

Please check **www.PacktPub.com** for information on our titles

Printed by BoD™in Norderstedt, Germany